UNESCO sourcebook for science in the primary school

A workshop approach to teacher education

Wynne Harlen
Jos Elstgeest

UNESCO Publishing

Published in 1992 by the United Nations Educational,
Scientific and Cultural Organization,
7 place de Fontenoy, 75352 Paris 07 SP

Composed by UNESCO Publishing
Printed by Imprimerie de la Manutention, Mayenne

ISBN 92-3-102721-2

Preface

This UNESCO sourcebook has been prepared as a supplement to the *Unesco Handbook for Science Teachers*[1] and the *New Unesco Source Book for Science Teaching*.[2] It is part of UNESCO's contribution to the efforts by various organizations and Member States to improve science teaching, especially at the primary level.

The origins of this book go back to the early 1980s when the Committee on the Teaching of Science of the International Council of Scientific Unions (ICSU–CTS) set up a Sub-committee on Elementary Science (SES). This sub-committee's discussions as to how to improve primary/elementary school science education led to the conclusion that primary-school science-teachers' training programmes as a whole did not provide effective preparation for teaching active and relevant science. In view of the priority that Unesco is placing on basic education, its limited resources would appear to be best directed to teacher educators.

The authors of this book, Jos Elstgeest and Wynne Harlen, were for many years the surviving and active members of SES. In the early 1980s the latter put together *The Training of Primary Science Educators – A Workshop Approach*[3] written by three SES members: herself, Jos Elstgeest and Dr Juan-Manuel Gutierrez-Vazquez of Mexico.

This book is divided into two parts: Part One, by Wynne Harlen, Director of the Scottish Council for Research in Education, deals with methods of teaching relating to a view of active learning in science; Part Two, by Jos Elstgeest, a specialist in in-service primary-school science-teacher training in

1. *Unesco Handbook for Science Teachers*, Paris/London, UNESCO/Heinemann, 1980, 199 pp.
2. *New Unesco Source Book for Science Teaching*, Paris, UNESCO, 1973, 270 pp.
3. Wynne Harlen (ed.), *The Training of Primary Science Educators – A Workshop Approach*, Paris, UNESCO, 1984, 91 pp. (Science and Technology Education Document Series, 13.)

the Netherlands, provides exemplary materials for classroom activities. The two parts are intended to be used together, not in sequence; their style is direct and aimed to encourage teachers to try the ideas suggested.

This publication is designed for use in workshops for teachers in either pre-service or in-service contexts. The word 'workshop' is used here as a short-hand way of indicating an active learning experience in which the learner creates meaning and understanding through his or her own mental and physical activity.

In preparing this publication, the authors have made considerable use of ideas and materials generated through national, regional and international seminars sponsored largely by UNESCO, the Commonwealth Secretariat and ICSU–CTS. However, the authors are responsible for the choice and the presentation of the facts contained in this book and for the opinions expressed therein, which are not necessarily those of UNESCO and do not commit the Organization.

Contents

Introduction

The origins of this book

Many international organizations and individual science educators from different parts of the world have contributed in one way or another to the production of this book. It might be said to have begun in the establishment by the Committee on the Teaching of Science of the International Council of Scientific Unions (ICSU–CTS) of a Sub-committee on Elementary Science (SES) in the early 1980s. Jos Elstgeest and Wynne Harlen were for many years the surviving and active members of this sub-committee, whose discussions as to how to improve primary/elementary school science education led to the conclusion that our very limited efforts were best directed at teacher educators, since primary-school teacher-training programmes were generally lacking in providing effective preparation for teaching active and relevant science.

With the support of UNESCO the SES prepared *The Training of Primary Science Educators – A Workshop Approach.*[1] A further activity was a brief International Workshop on Primary Science held immediately after the ICSU-sponsored Conference on Science and Technology Education held in Bangalore, India, in 1985, with support from UNESCO and the International Council of Associations for Science Education (ICASE) and the British Council. Then the Commonwealth Secretariat and UNESCO proposed to co-operate in taking the work further by launching a project whose aims were: in the short term, to bring together a small group of educators with expertise in primary-school science to plan a training workshop for teacher trainers and prepare draft materials; in the medium term, to bring together teacher trainers, mostly from Third World countries, for workshops using the approach exemplified in

1. Wynne Harlen (ed.), *The Training of Primary Science Educators – A Workshop Approach*, Paris, UNESCO, 1984, 91 pp. (Science and Technology Education Document Series, 13.)

the materials; and in the long term, to collect together and develop further workshop materials for use in pre-service and in-service courses and make them available to teachers and to those providing courses for teachers.

The first of these aims was achieved through a small international seminar convened in Liverpool in December 1986. The second was achieved initially through an international seminar held in Barbados in 1987 and attended by twenty-six participants from seventeen countries. The seminar was organized by the Commonwealth Secretariat and UNESCO, supported by ICSU–CTS, ICASE and the British Council and co-directed by Professor Wynne Harlen, then of Liverpool University, and Dr Winston King, of the University of the West Indies. The aim of the seminar was that participants would subsequently run national and regional workshops along similar lines, using the ideas and materials generated and used in Barbados. The realization of this aim took the form of two workshops in the Caribbean (one in Uganda and one in Malaysia), a South-East Asia regional seminar held in Western Samoa in 1989 and an African regional workshop held in Nigeria in 1990.

The value of the workshop materials has been evident in supporting these activities and the purpose of this volume, which is the achievement of the long-term aim of the Commonwealth Secretariat/UNESCO project, is to extend this help more widely. The present book is therefore intended for use in teacher-education courses – pre-service or in-service; it is best used when the activities suggested can be carried out and discussed by students or teachers in groups. However, the needs of the individual teacher, without access to in-service courses, have been borne in mind and the book can also be used for independent study.

In preparing this volume to cover more ground than was possible in the project seminars and workshops, it has been necessary to produce a considerable amount of new material. Many of the participants at the Barbados seminar will recognize their contributions, particularly Kamala Peiris and Sheila Jelly, whose work is acknowledged with great gratitude. However, the bulk of Part One of the book has been written by Wynne Harlen and of Part Two by Jos Elstgeest; Wynne Harlen brought it together as overall editor.

Intended use

The material here is designed for use in workshops for teachers in either pre-service or in-service contexts. The word 'workshop' is used to convey a particular active approach to teacher education which the authors feel is essential. The idea of active learning involves both physical and mental activity. Participation in the creation of ideas (even if others have already arrived at them) is essential to learning with understanding at all levels. This way of learning promotes the important feature of 'ownership' of ideas and is relevant to all learners, not just to children.

A workshop is merely a shorthand way of indicating a learning experience in which the learner creates meaning or understanding through his or her own mental and physical activity. What is provided as a basis for this action can be objects or materials to investigate or use, or problems to solve, or evidence to examine and discuss. The outcome may be an artefact, a solution to a problem, a plan, the recognition of a new relationship between things, a critique or a set of criteria. Perhaps the most important product, however, is a greater understanding of how to achieve such outcomes.

For teachers to understand fully the meaning of active learning it is important for them to have experienced it for themselves and so this is one reason for advocating a large element of workshop activity in a teacher-education course. To help children learn in this way it is necessary to understand, not just at an intellectual level, but in terms of practice, what it means to carry out observation, to hypothesize, to make a prediction, to plan an investigation, and so on. This is a tall order for those who may never in their own education have had opportunity to create and test a hypothesis based on their own ideas.

Further, not only do teachers and intending teachers need to experience these things for themselves but to do so in a context where discussion can turn to analysing the role of process skills and concepts in their learning, to reflecting on the sorts of activities which encourage use of these skills and concepts, to considering the teacher's role in these activities and to identifying the range of class organizations, strategies and resources which are required.

This way of learning does not have to be restricted to developing personal knowledge of science. It can and should be applied to all the learning experiences in a teacher-education course. It means starting from the ideas which are already present and working with the learner, making use of evidence (from previous experience and logical argument as well as direct observation, since we are dealing with adults) to change them. Working in this way has a double benefit in bringing about understanding relating to the nature of learning and at the same time being the most effective way for teachers to learn the skills and abilities required for effective science teaching.

The structure of this book

The two parts of this book are intended to be used together, not in sequence. The reason for separating them is to provide flexibility so that those designing courses can make whatever selection and mixture of methodological and practical elements which are appropriate for their particular purposes.

Part One deals with the methods of teaching related to active learning, which is explained in the first chapter, about learning in science. Through workshop activities ideas are introduced about how children gradually form a scientific understanding of their environment, the role in this of process skills, the identification of these skills and the importance of children's initial ideas as starting-points in learning.

Chapter 2 provides some directed activities in science and technology for teachers and students to try for themselves and then with children. These include 'fair testing' activities, simple technology and some hypothesis testing activities. Suggestions are given for how to organize activities for children.

Chapter 3 discusses the activities carried out in Chapter 2 in terms of what the 'doer' (teacher or child) did, pointing out the aspects which make the activity one of learning science. A check-list is presented for use in identifying the science in activities and deciding how these can be adapted to improve the opportunities for active learning.

Chapter 4 takes up the meaning of process skills through activities which are described as a 'process circus'. The discussion leads to suggested 'indicators' for process skills and attitudes.

Chapter 5 starts from the importance of developing process skills and attitudes. The general nature of progression in process skills is described, followed by suggestions as to how teachers can help this in promoting development in each of the process skills.

Chapter 6 links back to Chapter 1 and the discussion of children's existing ideas and the view of learning as change in these initial ideas. The development of children's ideas is described in general terms, highlighting the nature of progress and general strategies for helping children to develop their ideas in the direction of this progress.

Chapter 7 is about language and reporting in science. The importance of discussion among children in the development of their ideas is a theme throughout the book, but here it is examined more closely. The relationship of language and thought is explored through transcripts of conversations between teacher and child. The problem of whether and when to introduce scientific vocabulary is addressed and ways of finding out the meaning children attach to the 'scientific' words they use are proposed. Ways of encouraging children to communicate their thinking and findings in writing are also discussed.

Chapter 8 is about children's questions; the importance of asking all kinds of questions and discussion of those particularly useful in science. Workshop activities include categorizing questions and identification of the kinds of teachers' questions which encourage children to investigate and use process skills.

Chapter 9 is about using the environment outside the classroom for science, starting with the idea of an observation trail and providing guidelines for how to develop one in any school grounds. Ideas for more sustained scientific study of the natural environment are introduced and can be related to the material in Chapter 15.

Chapter 10 is the first of two on the assessment of learning. It gives a brief introduction to the principles of assessment in different ways for different purposes. It makes a case for assessment as part of teaching in terms of the importance of matching. Various methods are introduced for assessing children's ideas as part of normal classroom activities and for assessing skills and attitudes by observation. Attention is drawn to the importance of planning activities with assessment in mind.

Chapter 11 deals with formal assessment of scientific concepts and skills. Tests, examinations and other formal assessments need to be consistent with the objectives of active learning if it is to be genuinely practised. Examples are provided for critical study of written questions which assess understanding rather than recall and some process skills; ideas are given for developing such questions.

Chapter 12 gives further and more detailed attention to evaluating learning opportunities in science for all pupils. Check-lists are exemplified which teachers can use to evaluate the opportunities they are providing for active learning and the extent to which pupils are taking advantage of these opportunities. Particular attention is given to the provision of appropriate opportunities for pupils of both sexes, those of different ethnic backgrounds, and those with language and other learning difficulties.

Part Two of the book provides exemplary classroom activities which are intended to be used by teachers during courses as well as with children. Their use in teacher-education courses involves teachers or student teachers in doing some science activities, at their own level, but in the way in which it is hoped they will do science activities for their children. The experience of active learning is the only way for teachers or others really to understand what it means and, moreover, it invariably creates the excitement and enthusiasm for science which teachers require and which few have had the opportunity to experience in their own education.

Chapter 13 gives a general introduction to the use of the classroom activities, which are, of course, only intended to be examples, not a complete programme, on any of the topics. The concrete examples provide the best opportunity to discuss the pros and cons of worksheets and it is suggested that part of the engagement of teachers with the activities should be to produce and criticize worksheets of their own.

Chapters 14 to 17 each have the same pattern: a brief introduction followed by a number of pages which present activities in an open way which invites inquiry.

PART ONE

Developing understanding and skills for teaching primary-school science

Wynne Harlen

Chapter 1

About learning in science

Introduction

In this first chapter we discuss some of the central reasons for promoting active learning in science. It is most important for teachers to have a rationale which makes sense to them and explains to others why children should have certain learning experiences. This rationale relates to the nature of scientific activity, what it means to learn science and how learning is brought about. Views of these things have a profound influence on the activities teachers provide for children, how they organize and manage their classrooms, what role they adopt, the way they use equipment and materials, and the criteria they use in assessing and evaluating the success of the work.

To substantiate this claim, suppose, just for the sake of the argument, that a particular teacher's view of learning is that it is a matter of rote memorization. This teacher will provide learning experiences which expose children to accurate facts and encourage them to memorize procedures and algorithms. To do a good job of this the teacher will probably provide the information in digestible packets, each to be mastered before the next is attempted. The class will be arranged to optimize exposure to information from the teacher, from the blackboard and from books and to minimize interference from non-authoritative sources, such as other children. The teacher's role will be seen as to ensure attention, to present information clearly and to reward accurate recall; the pupil's role is to attend, to memorize and to recall; materials may be used to illustrate applications of facts already learned or simply to add interest and prevent boredom. Assessment criteria will be defined in terms of recall of information.

If the teacher has a different view of learning, where the learner is active in creating understanding and using process skills to test and modify ideas (as discussed later in this chapter), then the classroom provision consistent with it will clearly be quite different from that described for rote learning. Now the experiences provided will enable pupils actively to seek evidence through their own senses, to test their ideas and to take account of others' ideas through discussion and using sources of information; the organization will facilitate interaction of pupils with materials and pupils with pupils; the teacher's role will be to help children to express and test their ideas, to reflect upon evidence and to question the way they carry out their investigations; the materials have a central role in providing evidence as well as arousing curiosity in the world around. The assessment criteria must include reference to process skill development and understanding of ideas, and not neglect the development of scientific attitudes.

Both of these teachers provide a learning environment which is consistent with their view of learning. Many teachers cannot provide all the opportunities for their children which they value and would like to provide, but they find ways of minimizing the effect of the constraints on their work and they are aware of the shortcomings of some of the children's classroom experiences. It is the self-imposed constraints under which some teachers work – because of a limited view of science and of learning in science – which can be avoided. Thus it is important to begin by discussing the nature of learning in science.

Scientific activity

Science is a human enterprise through which we come to some understanding of the biological and physical aspects of the world around. This 'understanding' involves the development of ideas or concepts which enable related situations, objects or events to be linked together so that past experience enables us to make sense of new experience.

Developing concepts is an essential part of all learning, not just in science. If we did not develop concepts, then each new object we encounter would cause us a problem of identification; we would not be able even to identify a chair for what it is unless it was identical to one with which we were already familiar. But as it is we can recognize a chair we have never seen before as a chair, or a previously unknown living thing as living, or realize that something which seems to disappear in water has dissolved rather than vanished, because we already have ideas which help us make sense of these things.

Building up ideas about the scientific aspects of the world is the business of science and of science education. The ideas of science change as scientists extend their explorations and expose their theories to wider testing. In attempting to understand something new, scientists use existing ideas and test the extent to which they fit the evidence from the new situation or object under investigation. The result of this testing may be the confirmation that the existing ideas do fit and help in understanding the new observations, or it may reveal the need to modify or perhaps entirely reject the use of existing ideas because they do not fit new evidence. Similarly, in learning science the ideas that an individual has gradually change as experience and ability to reflect on experience accrue.

Before discussing children's learning, it is useful to examine a specific learning experience. Here is a problem to think about. It leads to some investigations which will involve ideas about light. Think out your reasons for the answers you give.

If you have a chance to do this in a group with others, exchange answers and ask others for their reasons.

THROWING SOME LIGHT ON LEARNING

Imagine there is a very small candle or taper burning in a large, dark room. As you gradually move away from it, it becomes fainter and fainter. At some distance, you cannot see it any more:
1. Would the distance at which this happens be the same if the room were lit up?
2. If not, would the distance at which you cannot see the candle be shorter or longer than when the room is dark?
3. If the candle were replaced by a small white ball (table tennis ball, for example), what would your answers be to these same questions?

Now try the investigation in practice. It needs a surprisingly small light source – no more than the glow of a cigarette. However, a healthier small source can be arranged by linking several small bulbs in series to a 1.2 volt cell and covering all but one bulb. The area where you work does not have to be completely dark; any place where the lighting varies or can be changed will do (even outside).

Have you found out anything which has changed your first ideas?

Think about things other than the ambient lighting which might make a difference to how far away the candle can be seen. First make predictions; say what you would expect to make a difference, what difference it would make and give your reasons.

Then test your ideas in practice.

Reflecting on learning in science

Reflecting on these and on other learning experiences which you may recall, you were developing greater or new understanding by testing initial ideas against evidence. If necessary, you changed your ideas so that they agreed with the evidence. Building ideas in this way is at the heart of science and of science education.

If we now change focus from the ideas about light to the way in which the ideas were tested and used, you will probably find that in these activities you have been:

- making predictions (saying what you think will happen on the basis of your ideas and previous experience);
- giving hypotheses (suggesting explanations for what you think will happen or for what does happen);
- planning and then carrying out an investigation to test your predictions;
- making observations (looking at what happens);
- interpreting observations;
- communicating with others about your and their ideas.

These are among the activities often described as the processes or methods of science. They are chiefly mental skills, but also involve some associated physical skills. They are concerned with processing evidence and ideas, and so are often called *process skills*.

Through using these process skills you may have clarified, queried, perhaps modified, or in other ways developed your initial ideas or concepts about light and how things are seen. This development is not an automatic process, however. What results from trying out ideas depends on the *way* in which they are tried out. If these processes are not carried out in a rigorous and scientific manner, then the emerging ideas will not necessarily fit the evidence; ideas may be accepted which ought to have been rejected, and vice versa. Thus the development of ideas depends crucially on the processes used.

In the case of children, we know that they often observe superficially, looking for confirmation of their ideas rather than being more open-minded and using all the evidence available; we know that their first attempts at prediction are really based on what they already know to be the case rather than being true predictions; the tests they carry out are often far from being 'fair' or controlled; they rarely check or repeat observations or measurements. Just as their ideas or concepts are limited and immature, so are their process skills, and both are capable of development.

The dependence of concept development on the way in which children are tested – that is, on the use of process skills – provides one part of the rationale for the importance of developing these skills. It cannot be too strongly emphasized that attention to developing process skills is not for any supposed value in their own right, but because of their value in developing concepts.

A second part of the rationale for giving attention to process skills is implicit in the type of learning just described, learning in which the learner collects the evidence and does the reasoning, making the ideas his or her own. This is what we may call learning with understanding. Learning without understanding, as in rote memorization, does not require the use of process skills. We need not linger long on the faults of rote learning, but it is worth observing that much science was (and probably is) taught in a way which leaves pupils little option but to learn facts by heart. This leads to science being regarded as a mystery, as not making sense and has nothing to do with understanding the world around, which is surely the aim of our science education. Moreover we want pupils and future citizens to feel at ease with science, to know its strengths and weaknesses, even if they are not practising science, and the best way of achieving this is through experience of finding things out and working out ideas.

We now consider at a theoretical level how learning, in terms of the development of ideas, depends on the way of gathering evidence and testing ideas.

The role of process skills in learning

We have just seen that the understanding of the world around depends on the development of concepts, but this development depends on the use of the process skills. The two are interdependent: as concepts gradually become more sophisticated, so process skills need to be refined and extended. Development of both must go hand in hand.

It may be helpful to represent the linking of ideas to new experiences by the following diagram. The circles I_1, I_2 and I_3 represent various existing ideas and E represents a new experience.

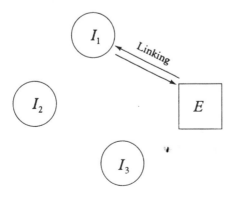

One of the existing ideas is linked to the new experience in preference to other possibilities because of some perceived similarities. The processes involved in this may include observing, hypothesizing and communicating (words often trigger links). The idea which has been linked is then tested against evidence to see whether or not it helps in making sense of the new experience. If it does, it will emerge reinforced as a more useful idea, strengthened by having a wider range of applications. But whether or not this happens, or whether the idea is found to need modification or should be rejected, depends on the way in which the testing processes are carried out.

The testing processes include raising questions, predicting, planning and carrying out investigations, interpreting and making inferences, and observing, measuring and communicating. In the figure below we have a simple model of learning in which conceptual learning is seen as the modification and expansion of existing ideas rather than the creation of new ideas. The process depends on the learners using and testing ideas they already have.

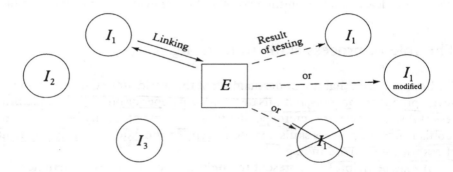

Which one of the possibilities represented in the diagram occurs depends not only on the existing ideas and the nature of the new experience, but on the extent to which scientific process skills can be used. Here we should also add that attitudes are also a determining factor in whether or not available skills will be deployed.

If we now think of the new experience as being one provided in school so that children can learn, then we see that process skills and attitudes exercise a determining influence on the extent to which conceptual learning takes place. The ideas and understanding which children achieve from an experience will depend on their ability to carry out the processes scientifically. But, like concepts, these skills and attitudes have to be developed gradually.

Objectives of learning science

The above discussion leads to a set of objectives for learning science which can be expressed formally as concepts, process skills and attitudes. It is useful to state these explicitly at the level of general statements which have universal currency, encapsulating what is essential to learning science in any country, any context and any culture. This is not to say that the learning activities of children are universal. Far from it; these should be devised or selected so as to relate to children's interests and everyday experience, to appeal to and develop their curiosity, to involve them in studying and trying to tackle real-life problems, and to help them understand their particular environment. Children should be developing these concepts, process skills and attitudes through such diverse activities.

THE CONCEPTUAL OBJECTIVES OF PRIMARY SCIENCE

The ideas children require to develop understanding of the scientific aspect of the world around are variously expressed in different curricula. However, when analysed they can be seen to fall under general headings of ideas about:
- the diversity of living things;
- the life processes and life cycles of plants and animals;
- the interaction of living things with the environment;
- types and uses of materials;
- air, atmosphere and weather;
- water and its interaction with other materials;
- light, sound and music;
- effects of heating and cooling;
- movement and forces;
- soil, rocks and the Earth's resources;
- the sky, solar system, planets and stars;
- magnetism and electricity.

The items in this list are not intended as a framework for constructing a teaching scheme or programme of work. Other points already mentioned (relevance to the children's environment, interests, etc.) will bear on the nature of the activities and the topics chosen for study. The items in the above list indicate what children should be learning about through those topics and activities. So, for example, the teaching may by organized around major themes such as:
- food and agriculture;
- health;
- traditional medicine;
- air;
- energy resources;

25

- preserving the environment;
- water;
- industry.

Basic concepts are developed through studies within these topics. Indeed the likelihood of understanding is far greater when ideas are studied in operation in something familiar and important to the children than if they are presented in isolation from their applications.

THE PROCESS-SKILL OBJECTIVES OF LEARNING SCIENCE

It has been found useful to express the process skills as in the format illustrated below. The layout avoids any indication of a hierarchy or sequence in the use of process skills. It also indicates that they are part of a whole, called scientific investigation. In action, it is often difficult to identify their separate use, but

the analytical approach helps in making provision for their development. This relationship to the whole process of investigation explains why 'investigation' is not listed as a skill – it is the amalgam of all those which are listed.

ATTITUDINAL OBJECTIVE OF LEARNING SCIENCE

A large number of attitudes can be seen to be relevant to active learning in science. Some of these that have been identified are co-operativeness, patience, honesty, cautiousness, open-mindedness, curiosity, flexibility in thinking and critical thinking. Most of these are of general value and not specific to science. Indeed the nature of attitudes is that they are generalized aspects of behaviour which describe a willingness to act or react in some way. However, we can recognize the particular value for active learning of willingness to:

- collect and use evidence;
- change ideas in the light of evidence (flexibility combined with open-mindedness);
- review procedures critically (critical reflection).

Chapter 2

Doing science: making a start

Introduction

This chapter is about teachers and children doing some practical investigative science and technological problem-solving.

Teachers who have not taught science before, or not much, or have not involved children in practical scientific investigations to any extent, may lack confidence in making a start on such work.

Generally one of the important reasons for this lack of confidence is that teachers have not experienced themselves the excitement and enjoyment of learning from one's own activity. Because of this, we begin with some science and technology for teachers to do. Later we will tackle other reasons for lack of confidence: problems of class management, resources, etc. But the essential thing is to have an understanding of what science activity means, an understanding which comes from within, and the knowledge which is created from first-hand experience.

The following four activities are for teachers to carry out *as adult inquirers*. There should be no attempt to pretend to be children, for the problems are real and are to be tackled at an adult level. Later the same activities can be tried with children and there will be some similarities and some differences in the way they tackle the problems as compared with adults. It will be interesting to reflect on these later in the discussion of scientific development.

Doing some science and technology

It is best to work with three or four others in a group if at all possible. Organize the group so that a record of your activity is made by one person and so that everyone is in agreement with what is done. Discuss all the ideas that are put forward and make sure that everyone has a chance to have their ideas tried out.

Except for Activity 4, use other equipment as well as that which is suggested.

ACTIVITY 1

Equipment: Pieces of four kinds of fabric taken from old clothes or left over from making clothes or other sewing, a candle in a sand tray, matches, stiff bare wire and clothes-pegs.

Question: Which of the fabrics is the least fire hazard?

The answer to this question is to be found by using the equipment and finding out how the materials behave. You will probably find that you need to discuss what is meant by 'fire hazard'. This is deliberately left uncertain so that you can consider different meanings and these may lead you to try testing the fabrics in different ways. The group should discuss and agree on each test and the necessary safety precautions before you do it. Don't stop after one test; see if different tests lead to different results.

When you have finished, prepare to report what you did and what you found to others in other groups.

ACTIVITY 2

Equipment: A piece of thin wood or card about 120 cm × 40 cm held in a shallow curve and three tins of food of the same size, with their labels intact, called A, B and C (A is a tin of soup, B a tin of beans and C a tin of meat).

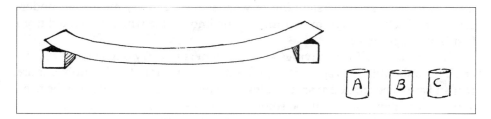

Question: Release tins A and B together from one end of the curve and watch them until they stop moving. Repeat with A and C and then with C and B. How do you explain any differences in the way the tins move to and fro across the board? Try to test out as many possible explanations (hypotheses) as you can and devise plans to test any which you cannot do with the equipment given.

Discuss how you are comparing the movement of the tins; there are several possibilities which may not necessarily give the same results. 'Brainstorm' all the ideas about why the tins move differently. Test out as many ideas as you can with the tins. Then devise a plan for trying out other ideas (or confirming ideas which you feel are satisfactory). Indicate in your plan what you would use (for instance, containers which you can fill with different things), what you would do with them and what you would compare or measure to find the result. If you have access to suitable equipment try out the investigation, but only after you have – as a group – agreed a detailed plan.

ACTIVITY 3

Equipment: None.

Activity: Go outside and find a small creature ('minibeast') in its natural habitat. Don't move or touch it except to make it easier to observe. Study it in the place where you find it.

Each person in the group should write down all the questions about the creature which come to mind. Then pool your list of questions and discuss each one. It may be that someone has made an observation which answers another's question, but if this is not the case discuss how you could find the answer to each question. In particular, identify those questions which you could answer by observing and exploring further the creature you have chosen. Decide what you would need to do; then, if you have time, go and find the answer from your minibeast.

ACTIVITY 4

Equipment: Some sheets of newspaper, a marble and a bottle top. No other material of any kind to be used.

Problem: Within the time-limit of 20 minutes, make the tallest structure that you can using the newspaper only. The structure must support the bottle top placed upside down with the marble in it.

The group has to make one structure meeting this specification. The time-limit has to be kept in mind so that the structure can be completed within the time available.

Discussion of the activities

In these activities you have been involved in scientific and technological thinking, learning and doing. You may or may not have been conscious of this, but hopefully you were conscious of enjoying the activity. Enjoyment is a powerful motivator and one which we should not neglect in teaching and learning. It is important to realize how enjoyable practical activity is; there is something particularly intriguing when thought and physical action are combined.

There are some other points to make about the activities as a group before we consider each separately. They shared the following characteristics: (a) they were all concerned with real problems or events; (b) they all used familiar and 'everyday' materials and equipment; (c) they all involved a great deal of discussion as well as action; (d) they could all be tackled in a variety of ways; (e) there were no instructions to follow – working out what to do and how to do it was part of the activity; and (f) each represented an approach which could be used with other subject-matter.

Activity 1 is representative of a range of activities concerned with making fair comparisons between things. Instead of 'Which fabric is the least fire hazard?', the problem could have been 'Which fabric is best for making a raincoat?', 'Which fabric is best for keeping you warm?', 'Which fabric is best for keeping you cool?', etc.

Instead of fabrics there could have been pieces of different kinds of paper, chosen appropriately for questions such as 'Which is best for soaking up water?' or 'Which is best for protecting a parcel?'. There could be a comparison of types of ball for their suitability for different games or a comparison of different kinds of wood for making a toy boat or a table. Leaves could be compared for their ability to keep someone cool and plant fibres for their usefulness in tying things together.

In all such activities there is an emphasis on 'fairness' in comparing one thing with another. Fairness in this sense means treating the objects to be compared in exactly the same way and not letting things vary in case they could be influencing the result as well as the difference which is being investigated. Probably you thought about this in testing the fabrics and took care to set light to them in the same way for all pieces tested, to use equal sized pieces, to test them in the same place so that draughts would not affect the way they burned, etc. In doing this you were controlling these variables, that is, keeping them the same so that they had no greater effect on one fabric than another.

In these types of problem, the words used are deliberately left slightly vague so that the particular property of the material has to be decided ('Which is best for making a raincoat?' rather than 'Which lets the least water through?'). Thus it makes the problem a real one and there is relevance to the finding out.

Activity 2 is again one of a family of activities. In these cases the starting-point is some phenomenon which can be observed easily and investigated practically, either using the same equipment or something devised to represent it. The emphasis here is on explaining what is observed. Often everyday happenings do not have a simple scientific explanation, but they are often amenable to an approximate explanation which fits the evidence and which is a step in the direction of a more sophisticated explanation. In many cases there are several possible simple explanations (hypotheses); by testing them out, the most likely can be identified.

In the case of the rolling tins you may have thought that the differences in movement were caused by the weight, a slight difference in size of the tins or something to do with the consistency of the contents. You could investigate these ideas to some extent with the tins given, but to find out which one(s) of these factors was making the difference it would be helpful to have some other containers which could be filled with different things.

The point of the activity is not, however, to understand exactly what makes the tins roll differently but to consider the possibilities, to recognize that there are several likely answers and to realize that investigation can enable one to eliminate some of them. This is the essence of scientific activity (as discussed in Chapter 1), in which understanding comes from refining ideas so that they fit the evidence.

Other common happenings can be investigated in this way, particularly by children whose ideas are uninfluenced by half-remembered 'right' answers as sometimes happens with adults (for example, the misting of a window-pane of a warm room when there is a sudden rainstorm).

Children will have many ideas about the reason for this which may seem strange but should be tried out by devising appropriate (and fair) investigations. The effect can be reproduced to order by putting some ice inside an empty food can (with the label removed so that there is a shiny surface).

Activity 3 illustrates an approach which can be used with a variety of different material. The prior step to extending knowledge is to ask questions. Questions identify what we do not know and so guide us to expanding our knowledge. Instead of living things the questions could have been stimulated, for example, by a collection of rocks, pebbles or shells, a bird's nest or a wasp's nest (found out of use) or an old tool or machine which is no longer in use. In each case the questions raised will range widely and will not all be answerable by scientific investigation. Later (see Chapter 8), there will be further discussion about types of questions and how to use them as a spring-board to investigation.

Sharing questions within a group is an important activity for the following reasons: (a) it shows everyone that they are not the only one who does not know, but wants to know, something; (b) it often leads to some questions being immediately answered by the observations which others have made, or from their prior knowledge; (c) explaining questions to others helps to refine ones which may not be clearly expressed (and this helps in seeking an answer); and (d) people are likely to be interested in the questions others ask as well as in their own.

Discussion of the questions in terms of how the answers might be found brings recognition that some can be answered by further observation and exploration. These are the questions with which science is concerned and it is important to distinguish them from other questions. The asking of all kinds of question is to be encouraged in learning; in learning science the asking of scientific questions clearly has an important part to play.

Activity 4 is different from the first three. It is not concerned with finding out or testing material but with solving a given practical problem within imposed constraints of materials and time. It is a *technological* problem. You will have used some knowledge of structures and materials in making your paper tower (for example, you knew that paper was not strong enough in single sheets but that stronger components could be made from it). You also had a well-defined goal and several constraints in reaching it. If you succeeded in making a tower meeting the requirements in the time given then you solved the problem, although you may not have made the most beautiful and sturdy structure possible.

The essence of technology is to do what is possible to solve the problem within the given constraints.

The essence of science is to reach the best understanding or explanation of certain events or phenomena consistent with the evidence.

There are many problems which can be devised to give experience of technological activity using the simplest of materials, for example, building a bridge from cardboard, making something which will allow an egg to be dropped to the floor without breaking or making a foot-operated device that will open a door. In everyday life, such problems do not have to be invented, they occur all the time and there always has been some technology to solve them. They also occur in scientific activity (for example, you had to solve a technological problem in arranging for the burning of pieces of fabric). Thus technology is important to science and science is important to technology (providing the knowledge to be applied). But the interdependence of science and technology does not make them the same. It is important for children to have experience of both types of activity and gradually to recognize the difference between them.

Working with children

Now try out with children at least the first activity and if possible all four of the activities described above. Make careful preparations beforehand but then do not direct the children's actions too closely. The organization described in some detail below for Activity 1 can be adapted for the others.

ORGANIZATION FOR ACTIVITY 1

If the children are too young to handle candles with safety, substitute one of the other questions suggested above. Arrange the children in groups (minimum three, maximum five). Introduce the problem to all the children by talking about the danger of inflammable clothing (or an equivalent topic if you have chosen another problem).

Take care about the following points:

- that the children all understand the words being used (use words which are likely to be familiar to them);
- that they understand the problem;
- that you move carefully from discussing the general problem to the problem that they are going to investigate (in this case to test certain kinds of fabric that you have collected);
- that they realize that they are going to find the answer by testing the fabrics (not by guessing which is best).

Before you distribute the equipment, tell the children to work as a group, sharing the work and discussing what they are going to do. They should also make sure that they keep a note of important things because they are going to have to tell others about what they did.

When they start work there will be a period during which they explore the fabrics and their activity may seem aimless, although they may come up with a quick answer to the problem. Allow time for this initial exploration; if there is a superficial answer offered, discuss with the group how they came to their answer, ask them for evidence, to show you what they did. You can then discuss whether their 'test' was appropriate, whether it was 'fair', etc. Insist that there is no competition and no race to be first to finish. Visit each group to observe the progress. If necessary, gradually move the activity on by asking, for example, how they are intending to test the fabrics so that the tests are fair and how they will compare or measure something which is relevant to the property being studied.

Let them carry out their tests, with due regard for safety.

Whilst they are doing this your role is to move from group to group, keeping an eye on progress, asking questions if you are not sure why something is being done. To help keep the groups on task it is useful to ask 'How are you going to . . . ?' rather than 'Have you done . . . ?'. But as long as they have a thought-out procedure, let them try it, even if you can see that it may not be very helpful. Later, in a discussion, you can ensure that they realize that they did not select the best procedure when you ask them to criticize what they did and to say how they might improve it.

Draw the investigations to a close by telling the children to prepare to report what they have done, giving a time-limit for this preparation. There are various ways of reporting and of conducting the discussion, depending on the resources available and the experience of the children (see Chapter 7). Each group might make a poster to display their work and put this on display for all to see. One group might then be asked to talk about what they did, responding to questions from other children (in later activities other groups will take a turn to report orally).

The discussion is an important part of the activity and should not be rushed or left out. It is an opportunity for the children to:

- reflect on what was done;
- learn from mistakes;
- hear about alternative suggestions;
- learn to gently offer and politely receive constructive criticism.

Organize the class so that the children can sit and see comfortably, and tell them the purpose of the discussion. Then ask one group to describe what they did and found, and invite others to ask questions of the reporting group. Leave any comments of your own until last and then start with a positive comment or some praise for the group's effort. Give the group members a chance to be self-critical, first by asking if there is anything they would change to improve the investigation if they were starting again. Do everything you can to build up their confidence in being able to find things out by their own investigations.

Chapter 3

What makes an activity scientific?

Introduction

Here we step back from the practical activity of the last chapter to reflect on what was happening with a view to identifying the essential elements which provide opportunity for learning science.

A check-list for reviewing activities

The following questions can be applied to any practical activity. Think of the activities in Chapter 2 which you did and ask yourself whether or not, at some point, you were involved in these things:
1. Handling and using objects and materials?
2. Observing events and materials closely and carefully?
3. Using senses other than sight?
4. Trying different things with the materials to see what happened?
5. Sorting and grouping the materials according to their similarities and differences?
6. Discussing what was being done?
7. Making some kind of record of what was being done?
8. Communicating to others what was done and found?
9. Comparing what was found with what others found?
10. Being busy and absorbed in the activities for most of the time?
11. Raising questions about the materials and the investigation?
12. Puzzling over something that was found?

The answer is probably 'yes' to almost all, whichever activity you had in mind. This means that you had experience of observing and manipulating materials, discussing and communicating about what you were doing and trying to understand what was found.

But these things happen in many practical activities which are not necessarily scientific. Answering 'yes' to most of these questions indicates that there was potential for scientific activity in what was experienced and to evaluate whether or not the potential was realized to some extent it is necessary to probe further.

So far the questions refer to processes of observation and communication and attitudes which are common to many practical activities. These processes and attitudes are desirable, and indeed necessary, for scientific activity but they are not specific to it. To identify more specific aspects – those which distinguish scientific from other activity – other questions need to be posed.

Ask yourself whether or not at some point in the activity you were involved in:

13. Raising a question which could be answered by further investigation?
14. Suggesting a hypothesis to explain something?
15. Devising a test relevant to the question being investigated or to another question arising during the investigation?
16. Identifying and controlling variables which had to be kept the same for a fair test?
17. Deciding what was to be compared or measured?
18. Attempting to make measurements using appropriate instruments?
19. Taking steps to refine observations using instruments where necessary?
20. Applying scientific knowledge or ideas?
21. Recording findings in a table, graph, bar chart or in some other systematic way?
22. Seeking for patterns or regularities in the results?
23. Drawing conclusions based on the evidence?
24. Comparing what was found with earlier ideas?
25. Justifying the conclusions by reference to the evidence?
26. Repeating or checking results?
27. Recognizing sources of error or uncertainty in the results?
28. Trying, or at least discussing, different approaches to the investigation or to part of it?

These further questions indicate some aspects which are characteristic of scientific inquiry. They go further than the previous list by asking about how the materials were manipulated (rather than just whether they were handled), what reasons there were for doing various things, how systematic and controlled the investigation was, whether steps were taken to obtain precise and reproducible results and, perhaps most important, whether scientific ideas and knowledge were being used and advanced.

USING THE CHECK-LIST FOR CHILDREN'S ACTIVITIES

Now look back on the activity or activities you have carried out with children and ask questions 1 to 12 in relation to what the children did.

It is quite possible that you did not find so many 'yeses' as you did for your own activity. If this is the first time the children have been given an opportunity to work with materials, then quite a few 'noes' would not be very surprising. An important purpose of using the check-list is to diagnose problems and improve learning opportunities. The following suggestions about possible reasons for a few 'noes' may help:

What was happening	Possible reasons
Children not handling materials	Were there enough materials? Did the children realize that they could touch and use them?
Very restricted observing	Were the children really interested in the problem given? Were they distracted by something else going on?
Few questions raised	Was more time needed for children to become absorbed and to realize what sorts of things they can find out through their own actions?
Not much discussion	Were they used to sitting quietly in class and being told most things?

Several of these problems require more time to be spent in practical activity and for children to be encouraged to use their own ideas. It helps, however, if the investigation is introduced in a way which motivates and interests them. It can be related to a real problem (the importance of using safe fabrics for babies' clothes, for example, or knowing where certain minibeasts live and breed) or to a challenge, which is fun, or to a question which has arisen in some part of other work.

It is very helpful to have an area of the class where a few things can be put for children to observe, play with and wonder about in their free moments. The teacher can encourage children to bring in items for this collection and can add to it materials and objects which set the scene for topics to come.

The aspects represented in questions 13 to 28 will not all be found in every activity, but they should become increasingly common in children's experience as they become more capable of scientific thinking and inquiry.

It should not be a matter for surprise or dismay if rather few of the answers to questions 13 to 28 were 'yes' in relation to children's first attempts at scientific investigation. There are no quick answers that will change everything at a stroke; indeed the whole purpose of this book is to help in this matter.

Purposes of the check-list

The intention behind suggesting the check-list as we have just done is not to pass judgement on an activity or experience but rather to diagnose what aspects of scientific activity are present and what require to be developed.

There are several other uses for the list and we will refer to it often in later discussion. Some examples of other uses follow:
- In relation to any activity undertaken by children it can be the basis for review and helping to answer the question 'To what extent is this activity scientific?'. In general the more 'yeses' the more chance for learning in science to be taking place.
- Where science is part of integrated studies or topic-based, it is all too easy for it to remain at the level of 'look and tell' or even for activities such as reading about science to be mistaken for scientific activity. Scanning the work carried out by the children in terms of the check-list will indicate the extent of scientific activity.
- In selecting activities, the list can be used whilst mentally scanning what would be involved when children were carrying them out; it can help in a decision concerning how worth while activities are in terms of their potential for learning science.
- In devising or adapting activities, the items indicate the sort of opportunities that have to be planned for inclusion in classroom work.

(There is further discussion of the process of evaluating activities, and the teacher's role in them, in Chapter 12, where a more detailed set of criteria is suggested.)

Selecting and adapting activities

In science there is always a dual purpose in any activity: the development of children's scientific skills and attitudes, and the development of their scientific ideas. Since skills can be used on any subject-matter, they are not a basis for selecting subject-matter. The choice of content depends on the ideas or concepts that are to be developed. The particular selection of concepts is often determined by the syllabus or curriculum to be followed. Although syllabuses vary, there is, as suggested in Chapter 1, a core of ideas which are widely accepted as basic and always included. Concepts about air are among these, so we take an example from this area.

First, carry out this activity which involves making a parachute. It is presented as it appeared on a worksheet for children.

Parachute
- Cut a 14-inch square from sturdy plastic.
- Cut four pieces of string 14 inches long.
- Securely tape or tie a string to each corner of the plastic.
- Tie the free ends of the four strings together in a knot. Be sure the strings are all the same length.
- Tie a single string about 6 inches long to the knot.
- Add a weight, such as a washer, to the free end of the string.
- Pull the parachute up in the centre. Squeeze the plastic to make it as flat as possible.
- Fold the parachute twice.
- Wrap the string loosely around the plastic.
- Throw the parachute up into the air.

Results. The parachute opens and slowly carries the weight to the ground.

Why? The weight falls first, unwinding the string because the parachute, being larger, is held back by the air. The air fills the plastic, slowing down the rate of descent; if the weight falls too quickly a smaller object needs to be used.

Now apply the items of the check-list to what you did.

How many items did you tick?

The exact number will depend to some extent on the context in which you were working, but it is probably four or five from items 1 to 12 and none from the rest of the list. It is useful to think why this is so – why is the activity so impoverished in opportunities for learning?

The instructions are necessary because the observations cannot be made without getting to the point of having a 'working' parachute, but from then onwards the information given deters discussion and recording and prevents the learners from using their own ideas because the 'right' explanation is given. There is no opportunity to try different variations of the design which may help in the understanding of the phenomenon. A potentially rich learning experience is narrowed to one particular idea. Instead, it could be the starting-point for discussing gravity, balanced and unbalanced forces, speed and acceleration, air resistance and the properties of different materials.

How can the activity be modified to make it a potentially greater learning experience? Here is a suggestion. It starts in the same way as before. Thereafter the questions and suggestions might be introduced orally by the teacher rather than on a worksheet. But here they have to be written down.

- Cut a 14-inch square from strong plastic.
- Securely tape or tie a string to each corner of the plastic.
- Tie the free ends of the four strings together in a knot. Be sure the strings are all the same length.
- Add a weight, such as a washer, to the free end of the string.
- Pull the parachute up in the centre. Squeeze the plastic to make it as flat as possible.
- Fold the parachute twice.
- Wrap the string loosely around the plastic.
- Throw the parachute up into the air (or drop it from a height if that is possible).

What happens? Does everyone's parachute do the same? What is the same about the way all the parachutes fall? What is different? Why do you think that is?

If you throw up a weight not attached to a parachute, does it fall as quickly as the one attached to the parachute?

Try it.

Discuss with others in your group why this might be.

Do you think that if the parachute is bigger, or smaller, it will make a difference?

Decide how you will compare how quickly different parachutes fall.

Keep a record of how quickly the different sizes fall. Try each one several times.

Look at your results and at what other groups have found. Do you see any patterns (one thing appearing to be related to another) in the results?

What about other shapes (real parachutes are not square!)? Some have holes in them. Some are made of different materials.

Try some of these and see how well the parachutes fall.

Plan your investigation before you start. Think carefully about what you mean by how well the parachute falls (is speed the only consideration?). Think what parachutes are usually used for. How will you measure this? How will you make sure that the investigation is 'fair' (that is, if you are investigating different materials, that any differences are due only to the material)?

Prepare to report what you have found to other groups. After listening to what they have done, can you think of how you might have improved your plan to obtain more accurate results?

Put your heads and your results together and suggest how to make a parachute which falls very slowly but goes straight down without swaying sideways.

What else might make a difference to the parachute's fall? Think about different weather conditions and find out how your parachutes would behave in wind or rain.

Try out any other ideas that you have.

Now use the check-list in relation to these revised parachute activities.

It will probably be found that a very large proportion of the questions can be answered with a 'yes'. This analysis should answer the objection that the time taken for the revised activities is so much longer than for the original. The point is that the learning taking place is also very much greater. Moreover, several activities of the original type will never provide opportunities for the kind of experiences required for learning science. A change in quality is needed, not more of the same. The learning time for activities of the revised kind is not more but probably less when several such experiences are considered, because (a) many learning objectives are being met at the same time and (b) what is learned in terms of knowledge is learned through exploration and testing in practice – it is supported by evidence from real things and so is learned with understanding.

Of course, because fewer of these kinds of activities can be encountered in class time, it means that they have to be carefully selected to provide maximum learning opportunity. This important matter is one we shall take up in Chapter 12.

Chapter 4

Science process skills and attitudes

Introduction

When children interact with things in their environment in a scientific manner it is through using *process skills*: handling, manipulating, observing, questioning, interpreting, etc. The more they develop these skills the more they can learn through their own activity and come to a real understanding of how the physical and biological parts of the world around them work. Process skills are thus the route by which children explore and gain evidence which they use in developing ideas. In Chapter 1 we have considered the particular role process skills play in concept development and concluded that if children do not interact with things in a *scientific* way, using process skills rigorously, then the ideas they form may not be scientific in the sense of not really fitting the evidence. For example, if a test is not 'fair' in comparing things with 'all other things being equal', then differences may be assumed to have a different cause than is in fact the case.

Here, then, we have good reasons for giving purposeful attention to helping children develop process skills. The same may be said of the scientific attitudes which were mentioned in Chapter 1 – relating to the use of evidence, flexibility and open-mindedness, and critical reflection. These attitudes constitute the general inclination to behave scientifically in gathering and using evidence. Without them the potential ability to deploy process skills may not be realized.

At the same time as recognizing the importance of these attributes, we have to acknowledge that, whilst there is general agreement about their nature, they are often ill-defined at the level of detail. Sometimes people use the term 'hypothesis', for example, believing that others share their understanding of it, although this may not be the case. At other times words such as 'conclusion' and 'inference' might be used interchangeably, whilst some may

45

argue strongly that they are quite different. Part of the problem is that these words have an 'everyday' meaning, not well defined, as well as a meaning in the particular context of science.

It would be too ambitious to suppose that we can eliminate these difficulties of usage and varying meanings by arriving at some universal definitions here. The more modest aim in this chapter is to *describe* process skills *in action* so that they can be recognized when they happen and so that teachers can work towards bringing about the ability to carry out these things in their pupils. We are concerned, then, with operational definitions – indicating, through describing activities and the experience of carrying them out, what it is one is doing when using process skills.

This chapter's concern with the meaning of process skills at experiential level is important as a basis for considering how to help children in their development of skills and attitudes, the subject of the next chapter.

Workshop activities on process skills

The series of short activities described below is designed to involve teachers in using process skills in practice. Performance of these, in a workshop context, must be followed by analysis and reflection, giving everyone a chance to change and develop, if necessary, their ideas about the meaning in action of the process skills.

It is vital that the activities be *experienced* and not just discussed in theory, so every effort should be made to carry them out. The equipment is simple and is described for each one, together with the instructions. The activities can be done in any order and starting at any point, so everyone can be moving round the 'circus' at the same time.

While carrying out the activities, which is best done working with a partner, decide which of the process skills you consider you are using in the activity. There will inevitably be more than one but it may be possible to identify which is the one most used and to give this a special mark of some kind in the grid used to record judgements. A grid such as the following should be drawn up before starting:

Process skills \ Circus item	1	2	3	4	etc.
Observing					
Hypothesizing					
etc.					

THE PROCESS-SKILLS CIRCUS

The equipment for each activity is described. It should be set up as indicated and the instructions in the boxes written on cards placed by the equipment.

---

1. Draw what you think the candle will look like when it is lit. Put labels on your drawing.
   Now light the candle.
   Draw it again. What is different from what you first drew?

Equipment: Candle in holder. Matches.

---

2. Measure the amount of water that drips from the tap in one minute.
   Work out how much water will drip away in one day.

Equipment: 10 or 25 ml measuring cylinder. Stop-clock or stop-watch placed near sink where tap is dripping at steady rate.

---

3. If you have three different kinds of soil, how would you find out which had most water in it?
   Describe the investigation you would do.

Equipment: none.

---

4. Put two pieces of Velcro together. Try to part them. Try with one reversed/ crossways. Draw four boxes and in them make a series of drawings that explain how the Velcro works.

Equipment: Two matching short (10 cm approx.) pieces of Velcro. Hand lens.

---

5. Place the two mirrors at an angle so that reflections of the stamp can be seen.
   Count the reflections and measure the angle.
   Change the angle. Count the reflections (images) again.

Repeat for angles of 30, 45, 60 and 90 degrees.
Can you see a relationship between the number of images you get and the angle between the mirrors (measured in degrees)? (Drawing a graph may help.)
Use your results to say how many images you will get at 9, 49 and 78 degrees. See how near you are.

Equipment: Two mirrors held vertically by being stuck in plasticine, placed with one vertical edge touching and at an angle. A postage stamp placed between. Protractor.

6. Squeeze the bottle and watch the 'diver'.
   What differences do you see in the diver when the bottle is squeezed?
   Try to observe these observations to explain how it works.

Equipment: Plastic drinks bottle (clear sides, at least 1 litre capacity), 90 per cent filled with water and with a dropper in the water weighted with plasticine so that it *just* floats, then sinks when the bottle sides are squeezed.

7. Put ice in the can.
   Look at the outside of the can.
   Write down as many possible explanations as you can of what you see.

Equipment: Clean, empty, shiny food can without lid. Small lumps of ice.

8. Take a strip of paper and hold it vertically with one end in the water.
   Watch what happens for about two minutes.
   Write down any questions which occur to you as a result of your observations.
   Review the questions to see which could be answered by investigation.

Equipment: Beaker or jar of water. Several strips (about 1 cm × 15 cm) of blotting paper or filter paper.

9. Look carefully at the twig.
   Try to find signs which show:

- how much the twig grew in previous years (look at the scars which go all round);
- what was there before the scars which don't go all round;
- what the buds will grow into.

Equipment: Twig with buds and scars, but no leaves or flowers. Hand lens.

10. Fill in the table for an investigation to find out whether the kind of surface on which the toy is put makes a difference to how far it walks.

What will be changed	*What will be kept the same*	*What will be measured*

Equipment: None essential, but a clockwork toy can be provided (the point is to *plan*, not to *do*.)

11. On a surface covered with paper a clockwork toy moves 7 cm given one turn of the winder, 18 cm for two turns and 28 cm for three turns. (Accept these results as if you had obtained them.)
Display these results in a form that will help you to predict how far the toy will go for four turns.

Equipment: A clockwork toy, preferably slow-moving.

12. The two pendulums are of different masses. Use them to see if the mass of the bob makes any difference to how fast a pendulum swings.
Are you entirely happy about the result and the way you found it?
If not, suggest ways for improving the investigation so that you would be quite confident about the result.

Equipment: A stand with a horizontal arm on which two fine threads are tied, forming pendulums – one with a large and heavy bob and one with a small and light one.

DISCUSSION OF THE PROCESS-SKILL CIRCUS

After each pair has completed the circus and a grid, it is important to have an extended and unhurried discussion which identifies areas where different understandings arise in the meaning of the process skills. The discussion can be organized around the results of one pair, which are displayed. Taking the circus items one by one, the judgements made are first justified by the pair who made them and then any differences from what others found are discussed. Alternatively one pair can report on item 1, a second on item 2, and so on.

Although the results are used as the basis for discussion, it should be clear that the purpose is *not* to arrive at a 'correct' categorization of the items but to uncover ambiguities and differences in the whole group's understanding of the meaning of the process skills. Two points may help to avoid the discussion becoming confused. First, often people take the activity beyond what was required by the card and then record what they did, say, in dissecting a bud on the twig or beginning to answer some the questions they raised about the water rising up the strips of paper. So that everyone can be discussing the same activities, these must be restricted to what was requested in the instructions. Second, it is possible to argue that 'observation' and 'communication' are involved in every activity, because it is necessary to read the instructions. However, to define the particular nature of these process skills in the context of science, they have to be used in a way which is related to gaining or communicating information for the inquiry in hand. Thus they should only be included when they have a particular role to play in processing information.

The first few items will take a considerable time to discuss because the problems of meaning will arise for the first time in relation to several process skills. Once these are settled, the discussion of later items is more rapid. At all times the purpose – arriving at an agreed understanding of the meaning – should be kept in mind; using the circus items is merely a device to bring about the discussion through shared experience of real activities.

Experience has shown that certain process skills are the most likely to be contentious. The nature of prediction is a case in point. Some predictions depend on the identification of patterns in data or observations (and so overlap to some extent with 'finding patterns and relationships') whilst others are made on the basis of less ordered experience. The important thing is that there should be evidence for the prediction, either in current or past experience, so that it can be sharply distinguished from a guess.

The nature of 'hypothesizing' generally leads to some discussion. It has to be distinguished from predicting in the context of everyday use such as 'my hypothesis is that it is going to rain today'. A hypothesis is a statement which attempts an explanation of an event or relationship. A scientific hypothesis is one which can be tested scientifically. Another feature is the quality of tentativeness; the hypothesis is a *possible* explanation. This feature is best brought out by encouraging hypothesizing in situations where there is more than one obvious and possible reason for something happening.

The question often arises as to whether these activities can be used with children. The circus is particularly designed for a teachers' workshop. Isolated activities of this kind are not consistent with children pursuing inquiries using their ideas and testing them out. Nevertheless, there are some aspects of the items which can be applied within the context of children's inquiries. For example, the notion of asking children to draw something which they are about to observe before they in fact look at it can be applied usefully in certain circumstances to focus children's attention to detail. Again, one of the difficulties teachers often encounter is how to arrange for children to raise questions; item 8 gives an example of how this can be done.

A useful outcome of the discussion of process skills is a list of actions which indicate that a particular process skill is being used. These *indicators* are valuable in many different ways:

- for teachers to use in observing their children and deciding the extent to which they are engaged in the actions that indicate that process skills are being used;
- for guiding the evaluation and adaptation of activities, where they can be the basis of questions such as 'Do these activities give opportunity for children to find patterns, to hypothesize?' etc. and then of changing the activities so that the children are likely to be involved in the actions described by the indicators;
- for suggesting how children can be helped to develop their process skills, as will be seen in the next chapter;
- for indicating the kinds of tasks that can be used to assess children's use of process skills (see Chapter 11).

The following lists of indicators have been drawn up in discussions as described above and should not be regarded as having any greater weight than this origin implies. The indication that they are unfinished is intended to underline this status. They are useful as a starting-point for teachers to develop their own lists.

Indicators of process skills

OBSERVING

- Using the senses (as many as safe and appropriate) to gather information.
- Identifying differences between similar objects or events.
- Identifying similarities between different objects or events.

- Noticing fine details that are relevant to an investigation.
- Recognizing the order in which sequenced events take place.
- Distinguishing from any observations those which are relevant to the problem in hand.
- ...

RAISING QUESTIONS

- Asking questions which lead to inquiry.
- Asking questions based on hypotheses.
- Identifying questions which they can answer by their own investigation.
- Putting questions into a form which indicates the investigation which has to be carried out.
- Recognizing that some questions cannot be answered by inquiry.
- ...

HYPOTHESIZING

- Attempting to explain observations or relationships in terms of some principle or concept.
- Applying concepts or knowledge gained in one situation to help understanding or solve a problem in another.
- Recognizing that there can be more than one possible explanation of an event.
- Recognizing the need to test explanations by gathering more evidence.
- Suggesting explanations which are testable even if unlikely.
- ...

PREDICTING

- Making use of evidence to make a prediction (as opposed to a guess which takes no account of evidence).
- Explicitly using patterns or relationships to make a prediction.
- Justifying how a prediction was made in terms of present evidence or past experience.
- Showing caution in making assumptions about the general application of a pattern beyond available evidence.
- Making use of patterns to extrapolate to cases where no information has been gathered.
- ...

FINDING PATTERNS AND RELATIONSHIPS

- Putting various pieces of information together (from direct observations or secondary sources) and inferring something from them.
- Finding regularities or trends in information, measurements or observations.
- Identifying an association between one variable and another.
- Realizing the difference between a conclusion that fits all the evidence and an inference that goes beyond it.
- Checking an inferred association or relationship against evidence.
- . . .

COMMUNICATING EFFECTIVELY

- Using writing or speech as a medium for sorting out ideas or linking one idea with another.
- Listening to others' ideas and responding to them.
- Keeping notes on actions or observations.
- Displaying results appropriately using graphs, tables, charts, etc.
- Reporting events systematically and clearly.
- Using sources of information.
- Considering how to present information so that it is understandable by others.
- . . .

DESIGNING AND MAKING

- Choosing appropriate materials for constructing things which have to work or serve a purpose.
- Choosing appropriate materials for constructing models.
- Producing a plan or design which is a realistic attempt at solving a problem.
- Succeeding in making models that work or meet certain criteria.
- Reviewing a plan or a construction in relation to the problem to be solved.
- . . .

DEVISING AND PLANNING INVESTIGATIONS

- Deciding what equipment, materials, etc. are needed for an investigation.
- Identifying what is to change or be changed when different observations or measurements are made.
- Identifying what variables are to be kept the same for a fair test.

- Identifying what is to be measured or compared.
- Considering beforehand how the measurements, comparisons, etc. are to be used to solve the problem.
- Deciding the order in which steps should be take in an investigation.
- . . .

MANIPULATING MATERIALS AND EQUIPMENT EFFECTIVELY

- Handling and manipulating materials with care for safety and efficiency.
- Using tools effectively and safely.
- Showing appropriate respect and care for living things.
- Assembling parts successfully to a plan.
- Working with the degree of precision appropriate to the task in hand.
- . . .

MEASURING AND CALCULATING

- Using an appropriate standard or non-standard measure in making comparisons or taking readings.
- Taking an adequate set of measurements for the task in hand.
- Using measuring instruments correctly and with reasonable precision.
- Computing results in an effective way.
- Showing concern for accuracy in checking measurements or calculations.
- . . .

Indicators of attitudes

Attitudes are more generalized aspects of behaviour than are process skills; indications of their presence have to show in a range of situations before they can be said to be present. We cannot, therefore, consider any one activity and say whether or not this or that attitude was involved, in the way in which we have done for process skills. In fact all the scientific attitudes identified in Chapter 1 may have been involved in all the activities of the process circus. Thus we cannot relate particular activities to particular attitudes.

However, we can still identify indicators of attitudes which can be used in much the same way as the indicators of process skills, except that they have to be applied across a range of activities rather than for any individual activity.

WILLINGNESS TO COLLECT AND USE EVIDENCE

- Reporting what actually happened, even if this was in conflict with expectations.
- Querying and checking parts of the evidence which do not fit into the pattern of other findings.
- Querying an interpretation or conclusion for which there is insufficient evidence.
- Setting out to collect further evidence before accepting a conclusion.
- Treating every conclusion as being open to challenge by further evidence.

WILLINGNESS TO CHANGE IDEAS IN THE LIGHT OF EVIDENCE (FLEXIBILITY COMBINED WITH OPEN-MINDEDNESS)

- Being prepared to change an existing idea when there is convincing evidence against it.
- Considering alternative ideas to their own.
- Spontaneously seeking alternative ideas rather than accepting the first one which fits the evidence.
- Relinquishing an existing idea after considering evidence.
- Realizing that it is necessary to change ideas when different ones make better sense of the evidence.

WILLINGNESS TO REVIEW PROCEDURES (CRITICAL REFLECTION)

- Willingness to review what they have done in order to consider how it might have been improved.
- Considering alternative procedures to those used.
- Considering the points in favour and against the way in which an investigation was carried out.
- Spontaneously reflecting on how the procedures might have been improved.
- Considering alternative procedures at the planning stage and reviewing those chosen during an investigation, not just at the end.

Chapter 5

Developing children's process skills and attitudes

Introduction

In the discussion of learning in science in Chapter 1 emphasis was given to the role of process skills in applying and testing ideas about the world around us. Through using processes such as observation, question-raising and hypothesizing, existing ideas are linked to new experience; through using process skills such as predicting, planning investigations, and finding patterns and relationships, conclusions are drawn about whether ideas fit the evidence. The way in which the processing is done is crucial to these conclusions, which in turn determine the extent to which there is progress in the development of ideas.

It is too simple to suggest that if children are given the opportunity to, say, plan investigations, they will necessarily develop their ability to plan, although undoubtedly opportunity is a vital first step. Planning, in common with all other process skills, can be performed in many different ways indicating varying levels of development of this skill. This has to be taken into account and encouragement appropriate to the point of development provided. In this way some progress is made in the gradual development of the process skill. The teacher has a central role to play in encouraging this progression.

Process skills develop gradually, as do concepts. It is the purpose of this chapter to describe this development and to indicate how it can be helped by the teacher. We shall also discuss scientific attitudes in the same way, since these are important, not only in learning, but also in enabling children to grow into adults who recognize the strengths and limitations of scientific knowledge.

The nature of progression in process skills

DIFFERENT WAYS OF DEVISING AND PLANNING AN INVESTIGATION

The following extract depicts ideas produced by some children (aged 10 and 11) when asked to plan how to find out whether their finger-nails or their toe-nails grew faster. Read the plans and try to arrange them in a sequence, from the one showing least development in planning skill to the one showing most. It may be helpful to refer to the indicators for planning, on pages 53 and 54.

Brian: To describe it I would cut my nails right down and see which ones would grow first, the quickest. That's how I would do it.

Lisa: You could keep checking your finger-nails and toe-nails for a week and keep all your information on a block chart; then at the end of the week you can see which grows faster.

Leroy: My test would be I would cut my finger-nails and I would cut my toe-nails and in a week or two I would see how long they have grown and if my toe-nails are longer they grow faster.

John: I would measure them each day to see which had grown faster.

Candy: At the beginning of a two-week period I would measure the length of my toe-nails and I would also measure the length of my finger-nails. At the end of the two weeks I would measure them both again and I would then know if my toe-nails grow faster than my finger-nails by taking the measurements of the beginning of the two weeks from the measurements at the end of the two weeks.[1]

It must be said that written plans will not necessarily reflect adequately the child's thinking, but these examples do at least serve the purpose of illustrating some of the characteristics of progression which apply across all the process skills.

Early stages in this progress are characterized by a somewhat superficial and almost casual approach, lack of specificity to the particular purpose of using the skill, and being unsystematic in its application. Development is shown by the use of skills becoming increasingly

- more systematic;
- more focused;
- more rigorous;
- more quantitative;
- more conscious.

What these general trends mean in terms of specific process skills is now con-

---

1. Wynne Harlen (ed.), *Primary Science: Taking the Plunge; How to Teach Primary Science More Effectively*, p. 58, London, Heinemann Educational Books, 1985.

sidered for each one. At the same time as describing the development, experiences which help to bring it about are suggested.

Helping children develop their process skills

OBSERVING

The reason for developing children's skill in observation is so that they will be able to use all their senses to gather information and evidence relevant to the particular investigation they are undertaking. There are two aspects of development of the skill involved here: attention to detail and ability to distinguish what is relevant to a particular investigation.

One of the early signs of development is that children notice greater detail than merely gross features. Their attention to detail has to be inferred from their actions as a result of their observation, since we do not have direct access to their sense perception. What children say, draw or write about what they see, smell, hear or taste, or feel with their fingers is an important source of evidence of their observation. Attention needs to be paid to these signs because simply giving opportunity for observation of detail will not necessarily mean that it has taken place. A sign of attention to detail is the voluntary use of some aid to careful observation, such as a hand lens.

A useful way of drawing attention to detail is to ask them to find differences between two similar things (two fish in a tank, or how a lump of sugar dissolves in warm and cold water). The converse question about two different things: 'What is the same about them?' should also be asked. Whilst there are always many signs of difference which do not necessarily have significance, the points of similarity between things can have more value in identifying them. Research with children has shown that finding similarities is rather more difficult and represents further development of the skill of observing than does finding differences.

Observations should be made for a purpose, however, and looking for similarities and differences just to see how many one can find is only a game. The opportunity to encourage attention to detail in this way is best taken within the context of a real investigation.

As experience increases it becomes possible for children to focus observation on that detail which is relevant to the problem. Knowledge from previous experience is required in order to know what is likely to be relevant. It is not possible, for example, to eliminate the colour of the plastic cover of a wire as having any relevance to its function in a simple circuit if you have never seen wires, bulbs and batteries before. This aspect of development of observing is, therefore, dependent on experience of a range of activities.

Putting objects or events into some sequence is also a way of focusing attention on relevant details. Encouraging children to make observations of things which change in sequence – shadows during a day and seasonal changes, for example – helps them to pick out certain features. Children also need to be helped to observe an event throughout and not just what happens at the beginning and the end. If they watch bubbles rising when they put water into a jar with some soil in it, or watch worms burrowing and making casts, they will be using their observation skill to give them information not just about *what* happens but *how* it happens.

Because there is always a tendency for us to see what we expect to see, it is necessary to become conscious of overriding the influence of preconceived ideas on our observation. To become aware of the way in which ideas can 'blinker' our ways of looking at things is a considerable step in progress. The level of development at which someone can reflect on the process of observation and consciously go beyond the focus of existing ideas is an aim which is probably not achieved in the primary school, although it depends on the foundations laid there.

Ways in which teachers can help progression in this skill include:
- providing opportunity (which means both materials and time) and encouragement for children to make both wide-ranging and more focused observations;
- arranging, through the class organization, for children to talk about their observations to each other and to the teacher;
- listening to the accounts of their observations and probing further ('What else did you notice?');
- providing, within the context of investigations, opportunities for children to observe events as they happen and use their observations as evidence in trying to explain what happened (developing hypotheses).

QUESTION-RAISING

Question-raising as a science process skill is concerned with questions which can be answered by inquiry; at the primary level these are questions which the children can answer by inquiry themselves or which they know can be answered by inquiry.

Raising investigable questions is important not just for the sake of being able to formulate and recognize such questions but, as in the case of all the process skills, because such questions lead to children's greater understanding of things around them. This understanding comes gradually through putting ideas and evidence together, prompted in the first instance by a desire to know, by a question. The clarity of the children's questions indicates the degree of their awareness of what they want to know and how it fits in with what they already know.

Whilst the aim in development of questioning skill in science is to help children raise questions which are investigable, the starting-point towards this is raising questions of any kind. To indicate too soon that science is concerned with certain kinds of questions and not others might deter the raising of questions. So we should see asking questions of any kind as a first step to progress in this skill. These may be questions which ask for names, for information, for explanations; they may be philosophical or may address aesthetic values, or they may be answerable by investigation or be capable of being turned into questions which can be investigated (see Chapter 8).

There are various degrees in specifying the kind of inquiry needed to answer a question. 'Is this kite better than that one?' is not strictly in an investigable form because it does not specify what 'best' means (although we can make a good guess). If the question is rephrased to specify that by 'best' we mean how high it flies, then it becomes clear what to look for (the dependent variable) to find the answer. It is already clear that what is being compared are two kites in this case and it is the type of kite which is to be changed in the investigation (the independent variable). It may well be possible to be more precise about what it is that is different about the two kites (such as the size or length of tail, etc.) and so to identify an independent variable which is a variable feature of the kites rather than the whole of each one.

When investigable questions are asked more frequently, it is likely to be because the children find them more effective, without consciously identifying how they differ from questions of other kinds. Becoming aware that some kinds of questions can be answered by investigation whilst others cannot is a point of progress. Once this difference is recognized, children may be able to go further and rephrase vague questions in a form that can be answered by investigation.

Children will readily ask questions in terms of 'how' and 'why' which are often not easy to answer: 'How do worms move without any legs?' 'Why are woodlice hard on the outside and soft in the middle?' In fact these are well on the way to being investigable and it may take little more than an invitation to say 'What do you think is the answer?' to set the children off to an investigation to see if their ideas fit the evidence.

Ways in which teachers can help children's progression in this skill include:

- taking children's questions seriously so that they see for themselves how each kind is answered;
- posing questions themselves in investigable form in science;
- helping children to clarify their questions so that they can see how to find an answer;

- giving invitations for children to raise questions ('What would you like to find out about . . . ?').
- Other strategies are indicated in Chapter 8.

HYPOTHESIZING

Hypothesizing is about trying to explain or account for data or observations, and involves using concepts or knowledge from previous experience. There are two important aspects which make a hypothesis scientific. First, it has to be consistent with the evidence: a hypothesis that a block of wood floats because it is light in weight but a coin sinks because it is heavy is inconsistent with the evidence if the block is heavier than the coin. Second, it has to be testable by collecting relevant evidence: the hypothesis about the block floating because of its weight is testable, but if the suggested reason were that it is suspended from an invisible, immaterial and undetectable thread, then it would be untestable.

There may be several testable hypotheses consistent with evidence, as in attempting to explain why one kite will fly higher than another (tail length? weight? shape? area?), and testing by investigation may eliminate some or all of them. Even a hypothesis which is not eliminated is still not proved to be 'correct' for there is always the possibility that it could be disproved by further evidence not so far collected. There is never enough positive evidence to prove a hypothesis correct but one (sound and reliable) negative test is enough to reject it. Thus a further characteristic of any hypothesis – any explanation – is that it is tentative and can be disproved.

Children do not naturally formulate hypotheses with these essential characteristics but there is a gradual progression in this process skill towards this direction. Identifying a feature of an event or phenomenon which is relevant to giving an explanation is a first step.

Connecting the phenomenon with a relevant idea from previous experience follows as the next step. Often this, as in the case of the earlier step, may involve only giving a name to something, not proposing any kind of mechanism which actually explains how it works or why something happens. For example, a stale slice of bread shrinks because it 'dries up'. This is hardly a testable hypothesis in the way described, but it is a foundation for further development.

The ability to propose a mechanism for the way a suggested explanation works is a necessary step in expressing a hypothesis in a way which is testable. If there is a mechanism which describes how one thing is supposed to relate to another, then this can be used to make a prediction. The evidence of whether the prediction is supported is then the test of the hypothesis on which it is based. If it is not disproved then it can be accepted, tentatively, as the best explanation, pending further suggestions and evidence.

Children's ability to propose mechanisms is naturally limited by their experience and ideas. They may on occasion put forward a hypothesis which is not possible, although they do not know this to be the case. Alternatively they may overlook what is to an adult an obvious explanation because they have not yet access to the relevant concept. However, as long as the explanation is testable, then we should see this as part of the development of the process of hypothesizing. With further experience, children will become more able to propose hypotheses which fit the evidence and are consistent with science concepts.

As the skill develops further the recognition of the tentativeness of hypotheses will show in children being able to give more than one possible explanation which is consistent with evidence and science concepts. These explanations may not be proposed formally as 'I think this is what is the reason for . . .' but may be expressed in questions posed or investigations planned and undertaken. 'Will the colours spread more quickly if we use warm water?' (in simple chromatography) is a question which encompasses a hypothesis. 'Let's see if the water disappears if we cover the saucer with cling film' similarly arises from a suggested mechanism, in this case for the water disappearing from a saucer.

Ways in which teachers can help children progress include:
- providing opportunities for children to investigate phenomena which they are able to explain from their past experience;
- organizing the class so that, when appropriate, children can discuss possible explanations with each other and so come to realize that there is a greater range of possibilities than they had first thought of;
- encouraging children to check the possible explanations against evidence and so reject the ones which are inconsistent with it;
- making available sources which children can use to find ideas to add to their own (such as books, visitors, pictures or films).

PREDICTING

The first thing to say about predicting is that it is not guessing. A guess has no rational foundation whilst a prediction makes use of evidence available, or past experience, and is related to this in some way. Children seldom make random guesses unless they are put under some pressure to give a quick answer and say the first thing which comes into their heads. Given a chance to think, they will make predictions which, in their minds, are justified by experience, even though they may not be able to express the connection clearly.

The extent to which children can explain the basis for a prediction is a dimension of progression in this skill. At first the prediction may appear to be unconnected with the evidence which was available, although the child did in fact take it into account in some unspecified way. Later the justification for the prediction may be articulated. Further development takes the form of being less rather than more confident about what can be predicted, indicating the realization of the risk of going beyond the evidence available.

Ways in which teachers can help the development of this skill include:

- encouraging children to make predictions and to justify them before carrying out the action or observation that will check their accuracy;
- discussing whether or not a reliable prediction can be made in a particular situation.

FINDING PATTERNS AND RELATIONSHIPS

The essential feature of this skill is relating one piece of evidence to another. The ability to do this enables children to make sense of a great deal of data which would otherwise be a mass of isolated pieces of information. However, to see the pattern in the association of one thing with another requires selecting the relevant features and not being distracted by others in which there is no pattern. Further, some patterns are consistent across all the data; for example, on a summer's day the position of a shadow will move steadily round in the same direction. The association between the time and the position of the shadow is so regular that it can be used to predict the position of the shadow at any particular time. On the other hand, the length of the shadow will first decrease and then increase during the day and so there is not such a simple relationship of length to time.

In other cases, whilst there is a general trend, there is no exact relationship. If we measure the foot length of people of different height, for example, there is a general tendency for longer feet to be associated with greater height, but there will be some who have longer feet than those who are taller than they are. Being able to identify overall relationships, despite the exceptions, is important in science and depends on taking account of all the information available. This is something which children appear not to do at first. They tend rather to see the extremes – 'the tallest person has the longest feet' – and not to look for the pattern across all the data. However, this is a first step in recognizing that one factor may be associated with another.

It is often difficult to know whether children who make a limited statement which seems to be only about part of the data have in fact noticed that all the data are related in the same way, but did not feel that the fact was important enough to mention. Only when the statement explicitly embraces all the data can we be sure that the interpretation is based on all the information available. In this case the statement is along the lines of 'the later the time, the further round the shadow is' or 'usually people have longer feet the taller they are'.

To be sure that there is a pattern linking one variable to another, at least three sets of observations are needed. It takes experience to realize this; perhaps learning from the experience of claiming a pattern exists from only two sets of information and then finding that a third set does not fit is the best lesson. This underlines the importance of checking all suggested patterns by making a prediction based on the pattern and seeing if the reality fits the prediction. Thus gathering further information to check interpretations is a considerable advance in the skill.

The help which teachers can give in this development includes:

- providing activities where there are simple patterns or relationships to be found in practice;
- asking children to express their ideas about relationships they think exist in their findings;
- requiring them to use any relationship they claim in making a prediction which is then tested;
- expecting them to check any relationships carefully and to be cautious in drawing conclusions from them.

COMMUNICATING EFFECTIVELY

Communicating is a skill which is applicable right across the curriculum and its particular role in science therefore has to be defined. It is included as a science process skill because of its role in developing understanding of the world around, in linking ideas to new events and particularly in reflecting on how these ideas relate to evidence gathered. Chapter 7 goes into more detail about the relationship between language, both spoken and written, and thought.

Recording and communicating are to be thought of in a far broader context than of producing a report at the end of an activity. Rather, both written and oral recording and communicating are integral parts of the activity throughout. Children need help in this, however, for at first they tend to make few records during an activity and inevitably are unable to recall all the relevant observations afterwards.

The development of skill in the area of recording and communicating begins with willingness to talk about all aspects of observations and experiences. Gradually, experience and teacher guidance enable children to organize the reporting of their work in science by presenting similar observations together, sequencing events and using simple charts, drawings and pictures to supplement words.

Extending the range of modes of communication requires some knowledge of ways of presenting information and of the conventions for using them. Once children have been introduced to the use of forms such as block graphs, flow diagrams, symbols, keys, etc., the development of skill shows in choosing an appropriate form in the context of a particular task.

Parallel with the increased use of graphical and written forms of communication is the continuing and important development of using words, in both written and oral forms, with accuracy and selectivity. Organizing a report so that events are described in a useful order becomes important when communication is genuinely used to inform others. Ensuring that there is a point in keeping a record – an audience for it – is a help in this respect.

Since communication is two-way, reading or listening to others' reports helps in fostering clear expression as well as being important in its own right for finding out about others' ideas and for contributing towards the understanding of written information and instructions. Written sources will increasingly be used for data, to supplement what is gathered at first hand, and the ability to interpret such data and search for patterns in it is an indication that the form in which it is presented is well understood.

The gradual increase in the meaningful use of scientific vocabulary is part of progression in the skills of recording and communicating. The use of specific scientific words is necessary since, as ideas become more advanced, they become more abstract and widely applicable (see Chapter 6); when referring to a solid in a liquid, the word 'disappear' has to be replaced by 'dissolve' in order to cover the range of effects which may occur; 'vibration' must gradually replace 'move up and down' because vibration can be in all directions; and 'conductor' is a very useful word to describe the invisible property of all the different substances which allow electricity to flow through them. The introduction of a new word has, of course, to coincide with the development of the idea which it labels, for the use of technical words without meaning is an obstacle to communication.

The help which teachers can give in the development of this skill includes:
- organizing the class so that children can talk about their work to each other, sometimes informally and sometimes reporting more formally;
- introducing a range of techniques for recording and communicating, using conventional forms and symbols;
- encouraging children to discuss and plan how their work will be best recorded and communicated to others;
- providing opportunities for children to use information presented in the form of tables, charts and graphs.

DESIGNING AND MAKING

Designing and making are technological skills required to bring about change through the application of knowledge and resources. Technology is an activity which uses knowledge and resources to make things work, control things and improve the way they work. Often the knowledge which is applied in technology is scientific or mathematical, and this gives technology a special relationship with these subjects. Technology draws upon scientific knowledge in designing solutions to practical problems and in making artefacts to meet certain needs. At the same time it contributes in providing systems and instruments which further the advance of scientific knowledge. However, there are times when technology draws upon knowledge and skills from other subjects, for example, art, geography and history, and so it has a link not only to science but also to subjects across the curriculum.

In primary school, children are involved in technological activity when they solve problems encountered in various areas of their work and play. They may want to build something for imaginative play (a 'den' or a house in a tree) or scale a wall, to build a model or make a rig for testing certain properties of materials. In all these activities they are involved in observing and investigating in relation to a problem, designing a possible solution, creating the artefact or system which has been designed and evaluating its effectiveness. Clearly some of these components of technology involve science process skills which we have discussed earlier. Here we are concerned with the development of the skills of identifying a problem, creating a design, making it and evaluating it.

Young children are beginning to identify needs when, for example, they suggest ways of rearranging something in the classroom for the better convenience of those who need to use it. As they progress in this capability they become able to suggest changes in less familiar situations and to consider the pros and cons of possible changes. Progress in designing shows in the reasons they are able to give for what they propose. At first these reasons will be vague with only an intuitive notion that they will work. Later, reasons will be in terms of the properties of the materials chosen and one design might be compared with another in these terms. Obviously this development is linked to increasing knowledge of materials and how they behave.

Constructing simple things from paper, glue, cardboard boxes and other scrap material is the start of developing capability in 'making'. Progress shows in the more careful choice of materials and precise use of tools. At all stages children evaluate their products, at first in terms of what they like and dislike about a model, then gradually focusing judgements on to the extent to which the original intention has been realized. Where appropriate they may make measurements to assess how far a solution meets certain criteria and then use the findings to suggest improvements.

Teachers can help the progress in designing and making skills by:
- providing opportunities for children to suggest changes in things around which will improve their use or solve a problem;
- requiring children to plan how to produce a model or some other artefact and discuss how realistic it is;
- providing a range of materials and the opportunity to explore their properties;
- providing problems which are interesting for children to solve and which they are expected to solve for themselves;
- expecting children to justify their choice of materials and to evaluate how effective they were in practice.

DEVISING AND PLANNING INVESTIGATIONS

Planning an investigation involves turning a question or a hypothesis into action designed to provide an answer. Although logically it may be thought to precede action, in reality the two are often closely intertwined. Younger children, for example, may not be able to think through a series of actions which could be considered as a plan; they need to see what happens as a result of the first step they think of before working out what to do next. It takes experience of investigations, of doing things and of seeing what happens before the possible outcomes of action can be anticipated and forward planning becomes possible.

The notion of 'fairness' is a useful one, as a way into considering variables. There are three kinds of variables to be considered in an investigation: the variable to change so that a difference between things or conditions can be investigated (the independent variable); the variables which must not be changed but must be controlled and kept the same throughout so that the effect of changing the one independent variable can be investigated (the control variable); the variable which is affected as a result of changing the independent variable and which is measured or compared in the investigation (the dependent variable).

In the common type of investigation where different materials are compared in terms of some property, for example the comparison of fabrics for waterproofness, the type of material (fabric) is the independent variable and the variables to be controlled depend on how the test is to be carried out. For example, if the fabrics are to be tested by placing water on the surface and seeing how long it takes to soak in, then it is important to use the same amount of water on each one and to apply it in the same way (two of the variables to be controlled). What is measured is the time taken for the drops to no longer stand on the surface. If the fabrics were compared, alternatively by seeing how *much* water each will soak up, then it would be important to use the same area of fabric (a variable to be controlled); the dependent variable would be the amount of water in each piece, probably measured by the difference between the water added and what was left after soaking the fabric.

Not surprisingly, children find the earlier parts of an investigation the easiest to plan. They can decide what to change – the independent variable – quite readily because this is often clear in the hypothesis or question under investigation: 'Which is the best fabric . . .' immediately suggests trying different fabrics.

As soon as they begin to think of how to proceed with the investigation, however, the matter of fairness will arise. Several unfair tests may well have to be experienced before the understanding of needing to control variables develops in a general way. It is certainly best for children to realize through the inconclusiveness of 'unfair' testing that certain things have to be kept the same. Attempts to teach control as a procedure often result in a tendency for children to think that they have to control everything, including the independent variable!

It seems that deciding how to arrive at the result of an investigation is more difficult than planning how to set up conditions to test the independent variable. Children are at first very vague about how they will find a result of an investigation. In testing food preferences of 'minibeasts', for example, they think as far as 'see how they like each food' as if this would in some way be obvious. Ideas about measuring time spent on the food, or amount eaten, come only when the impossibility of judging what small creatures 'like' is borne on them in practice. Thus precision in identifying what to measure or compare represents an advance in the process skill of planning. Further defining how to measure the dependent variable to an appropriate degree of accuracy is also a sign of this development.

Ways in which teachers can help children in the development of these skills include:

- leading children to problems which can be investigated but not giving them instructions for what to do, so that the children have to do the planning for themselves;
- helping the children to plan by giving some structure, perhaps through questions about what has to be kept the same for fairness, what is to be changed and what is to be measured;
- discussing plans with them and helping them to think through what they mean in practice;
- reviewing investigations after they have been completed to consider how the planning could have been improved.

MANIPULATING MATERIALS AND EQUIPMENT EFFECTIVELY

It is widely acknowledged that the two most significant factors which influence the intellectual development of young children are the availability of materials to explore and manipulate, and social interaction with adults and other children. In relation to scientific development, materials and things to explore them with are essential, not optional.

Learning in science involves children advancing their ideas by trying them out in practical investigations. The limited experience of children means that their ideas will not be the same as the accepted scientific ones, but they should be consistent with the evidence available to the children at any time (see Chapter 6). As this experience widens, ideas become more generally applicable and approach the scientific view. Thus the development of ideas is highly dependent on practical activity, involving the exploration of materials.

Children's limited experience also means that they are restricted in abstract and theoretical thinking; things have to be encountered in reality before they can be the subject of thought and mental manipulation. Thus the provision of this experience of objects and events around them is essential to their mental development. Its value is not only in terms of giving information through the senses about the world around, but also the realization that investigation can provide answers and that they themselves can learn from their own interaction with things around them.

It is not possible to distinguish practical activity from mental activity and we are therefore concerned with far more than the physical manipulation of objects and the ability to use equipment effectively. Practical activity must involve planning based on hypothesizing and prediction, gathering of information by observation and perhaps by measurement, the control of variables, interpretation of data, and the recording and communication of results. In each of these there is a combination of mental and physical activity.

It has to be understood, therefore, that in focusing on the physical development here, a context of social experience and mental activity is assumed.

Young children entering school have difficulty in small-muscle control and eye–hand co-ordination. They like to draw, paint, pull things apart, pile things up and knock them down. They need plenty of cardboard boxes of different sizes, cardboard tubes, egg boxes and newspaper to paint on with large brushes. If large wooden and plastic blocks are available, these are ideal, but where this is not the case, items of junk from home can be adapted.

To help develop children's small-muscle control and eye–hand co-ordination, their natural tendency to make models can be exploited. From a start of building with boxes or wooden blocks, they can begin to make more representational models, still using discarded materials that may be available from home, shops or the market. Egg boxes, plastic cups, plasticine and glue will come into use in making models. Other materials which are required and which can be obtained at no cost are things such as seeds, shells, rocks, cones and dried grasses. These can be handled and explored by the children, extending their awareness of the variety of natural things in their environment.

Children aged 7 to 9 have developed good eye–hand co-ordination; they can weave, sew, handle animals gently and plant seeds accurately. Their models will become more sophisticated; they will want to make them 'work', which often means greater accuracy and choice of materials. The use of tools becomes important. Children of this age can be shown how to use a hammer, saw, file and drill properly. A vice is essential for woodwork and children should never be allowed to hold in their hands wood which is being sawed, hammered or drilled. These aspects of safety do have to be enforced by rules, but at the same time the children should be encouraged to recognize potential danger and discuss how to do things safely, so that they are obeying rules which make sense to them.

There will also be an increased need for measuring instruments, and for hand lenses and more delicate equipment such as magnets, bulbs and mirrors. As with tools, when these are introduced, the precautions which have to be taken to preserve them should be discussed and agreed. The greater the freedom allowed to children to use their own ideas in investigations, the more responsibility they have to accept for the equipment they use. It is part of the teacher's role to ensure that these things go hand in hand.

At the upper end of the primary school, physical development is no longer a restraint on the use of equipment, but skill and care continue to be built up. For those fortunate enough to have microscopes and accurate balances in the school, the range of children's observation and investigation can be greatly increased. However, children can learn much, as well as being productive, through making a considerable amount of equipment for themselves. They will certainly be able to construct suitable housing for living things being studied, make simple balances, test rigs, etc.

They will also be able to make articles for younger children, such as wooden building blocks. However, there must be a strict limit on the amount of time which children devote to repetitive work with materials for the sake of production. Solving technological problems and learning about the properties of materials and control of energy in constructing something is one thing, but mass production is another. In science lessons, the manipulation of materials and equipment must serve the end of greater understanding, not the manufacture of products.

In summary, the ways in which teachers can help this development include:
- providing materials for exploration and use suited to the physical development of the children;

- encouraging children to extend their activity towards construction and the improvement of their constructions;
- showing children how to use equipment and tools effectively, economically and safely, and discussing reasons for rules of use but insisting on adherence to them;
- helping children to become conscious of how they can obtain answers to their questions through the manipulation of materials, thus encouraging them to persevere in developing the skills which are required.

MEASURING AND CALCULATING

One of the overall signs of progress in scientific processes which has been mentioned is that they have an increasingly quantitative element. This means that measuring and calculating will be called upon to a progressively greater extent.

Quantification means using numbers in a particular way. For example, numbers can be used merely as labels, as in the case of the numbers on the jerseys of football players, or as ways of placing objects in a sequence according to some feature or property, such as one being longer, shorter, hotter or faster, than the next.

When the differences between one item and another are quantified, it is possible to tell how much one thing is longer, shorter, hotter or faster than another and then relationships can be refined, patterns identified and predictions made from them.

The basis for saying 'how much' needs to be in terms of some uniform unit, but this need not be a standard unit. If children are introduced to measurement through standard procedures and units, they may be less likely to understand what a quantity actually means than if they can take the first steps by using arbitrary or non-standard units which they choose themselves – floor tiles for how far a wind-up toy travels, bricks in a wall for comparing heights, hand spans, strides, etc. The understanding of the nature of a measurement as being a multiple of a given unit can be grasped in this way. It soon becomes obvious that there is a need to keep the unit the same, that is, to use the same brick wall to compare heights in terms of bricks, or have the same person striding over distances to be compared and that a more convenient way is to use standard units such as metres, which mean the same everywhere.

Whether the unit is arbitrary or standard, however, it has to be appropriate to the size of the quantity being measured. It is inappropriate to measure the mass of a paper clip in kilograms or a person's height in kilometres. The choice of unit is tied to the instrument for measuring it and experience of various instruments for measuring quantities of mass, time, length, volume and temperature has to be acquired for children to be able to select an appropriate measuring instrument and use it with the degree of accuracy which is required.

As the observations and relationships with which children become concerned become more detailed and precise, so the measurements they make need to be more accurate. Accuracy comes only partly from the skill of using a measuring instrument carefully; it also depends on the procedures adopted, such as how many different measurements are taken and how many times each measurement of the same thing is repeated.

Arranging to take an adequate set of measurements is part of planning an investigation so that the range of variation in the independent variable is thoroughly investigated. For example, if the investigation is about the effect of temperature on how quickly substances dissolve, the result is unlikely to be conclusive if only cold and slightly warm water is used. A greater range of temperatures, and a least three different ones across this range, need to be used. Planning to take measurements across an adequate range indicates a development in understanding of the role of measurement in investigations.

In addition, the accuracy of each measurement has to be appropriate. It is as unhelpful to measure something to a high degree of accuracy beyond that required as it is to leave a great deal of uncertainty about the value because a measurement is rough. Accuracy can be improved to a certain extent by careful use of instruments but this cannot avoid the inevitable errors which arise in investigations and are inherent in measurement. Recognizing, for example, that the time taken for a certain mass of a substance to dissolve at a particular temperature will not be exactly the same if the test is repeated and that therefore repeating measurements will reduce the error represents a quite sophisticated level of development of the process skill of measurement.

From this discussion it is clear that there is a considerable knowledge base required for the development of this skill; there are conventions and procedures of measurement which have to be known and the appropriate deployment of these is an important dimension of progression.

Ways in which teachers can help this progression include:
- encouraging children to quantify their observations by questions such as 'How much more . . . is this than that?';
- providing questions for investigation which require measurement (for example: 'How much water does a potted plant require in a week?');
- providing a range of instruments for a particular quantity (such as a long measuring tape or rope, a metre rule divided into decimetres, a ruler in cm and mm and a micrometer, if possible);
- discussing with children the accuracy of their measurements and how to increase this, when it is appropriate to do so.

Helping children develop scientific attitudes

As we have said above, attitudes refer to generalized aspects of behaviour and are identified in the patterns in how people act and react in various situations. One instance of someone being willing to change his or her mind in the face of evidence is not a sufficient basis for judging them to be 'open-minded', but if this happens quite regularly it might well justify such a judgement.

Certain general characteristics of attitudes suggest the ways in which they can be fostered:

1. Attitudes are not things that children can be instructed in, for they are different to knowledge and skills. They exist in the way people behave and are transferred to children by a mixture of example and selective approval. Rather than being 'taught', attitudes are 'caught'. Thus an important way in which teachers can help children to develop attitudes is by *setting an example*. Thus if teachers, in their behaviour, show the characteristics described by the indicators of attitudes (see page 54), then they will be helping children to do develop these attitudes.

2. Attitudes are developed from what is approved and disapproved. Thus it is important to reinforce the signs of desired attitudes in what children do by praise and approval and to discourage negative attitudes in some appropriate way. If this is done consistently it eventually becomes part of the classroom climate and children may well begin to reinforce the attitudes for themselves and for each other.

3. Attitudes show in willingness to act in certain ways. Thus for children to develop these attributes there has to be the possibility for them to exercise choice. If their behaviour is closely controlled by rules and procedures, and they are always told what to do and to think, then there will be little opportunity to develop and demonstrate attitudes. For example, if children are never expected or encouraged to reflect critically on their work, it is unlikely that they will develop 'willingness to review procedures critically'. Thus teachers must *provide opportunities for children to exercise choice* in order to foster their development.

4. Attitudes are highly abstract and thus difficult to discuss with children. This is the reason why attitudes have to be encouraged by example and selective approval. However, as children become more mature they are more able to reflect on their own behaviour and motivations.

Discussing examples of, say, flexibility in thinking, will then help children to identify this attribute more explicitly rather than only implicitly from what is approved or disapproved. Care has to be taken that this approach does not become 'brainwashing', and a light touch is required. It can, however, help children to take responsibility for this part of their learning if they know what it is that they are aiming for.

Chapter 6

Development of children's science concepts

Introduction

In Chapter 1 we described children's learning as the change in ideas, brought about by the use of process skills. These skills enable initial ideas to be linked to new experience and to be tested against new evidence. This view of learning acknowledges that children do not come to their science activities with empty heads, but with ideas which they have formed in earlier activities and observations, and which they use in trying to make sense of the new phenomena they encounter as their experience expands. Sometimes the ideas which are used are not helpful (not 'scientific'), as when children might use the observation of drops of sweat forming on the skin when a person is hot to explain why drops of water appear on the surface of a cold can of drink when it is put in a warm room (the metal 'sweats').

The notion of the development as *change* in ideas, rather than as putting new ideas in place without consideration of anything already there, has important implications for how we go about helping this development. Furthermore, if we value the notion of children 'owning' their ideas, that is, working them out and changing them for themselves so that they learn with understanding, then this too means that teachers should be providing certain kinds of opportunities for these changes to take place in a way which gives the child this ownership.

This chapter describes some strategies which teachers can use to help this process of developing concepts whilst ensuring that the ideas make sense to the children. First, however, it is necessary to have in mind a clear idea of the general features of what we would call the development of progression in concepts. For it is only with this as a guide that a teacher can use the strategies to ensure that changes are in the general direction of this progress.

Thinking about progression

Some children were engaged in a range of activities about making sounds. They plucked stretched rubber bands, blew across the tops of bottles, tapped pieces of metal, banged a drum and then made as many sounds as they could using things around the room. They were challenged by the teacher to try to make a soft sound and a loud sound from each source they found; they also tried to change the pitch of the sound if they could.

Whilst they were working, the children made many comments about what they found. Below are some examples. Read them and then try to arrange them in an order which indicates a progression in ideas about sound. It is best to work in a small group with others if possible because then it will be necessary to explain why you wish to place the statements in a particular order. But in any case, make sure you do think about the reason for your decisions.

1. A drum makes a sound when you hit it. The sound is made by the banging.
2. When you pluck the rubber band you can see it vibrate and it makes the air vibrate into your ear.
3. I can make a louder sound by pulling the rubber band out further so it makes big vibrations.
4. You can hear the school bell outside when the door is closed because the sound comes through the gaps round the door.
5. I can hear someone tapping on the pipe if I put my ear on it but not if I don't. The sound comes through the metal.
6. A triangle makes a sound because it is metal and the right shape.
7. The little pieces of metal on the xylophone vibrate when you hit them and then the vibrations turn into sound.
8. I think you get high and low notes according to whether the thing vibrates quickly or slowly.
9. I can make the sound quieter by putting my hands over my ears.

You may find that, in order to do this, you need to think about just what are the main ideas about sound that we want children to develop. For primary-school children these ideas will probably not go much beyond realizing that:

- sounds are produced when objects vibrate;
- sounds are heard when the vibrations reach our ears;
- sound can travel through different materials and the frequency of vibration affects the pitch of the sound.

General characteristics of progression in scientific ideas

As children change their ideas, through modifying them so that they fit the evidence better or adopting alternative ideas, there is a general trend for the ideas to become:
- more widely applicable to a variety of related phenomena;
- more abstract, more complex;
- more precise and quantitative.

What this means will take different forms for different ideas, of course, but these general characteristics of progress can be seen as common across concepts. Some examples will be given as we consider these features in a little more detail.

IDEAS BECOMING MORE WIDELY APPLICABLE AND LINKING MORE RELATED PHENOMENA TOGETHER

Children tend to develop ideas which explain particular events without connecting them with ideas about other events which are in fact related. For example, the same child can explain the 'disappearance' of water (when it evaporates) in different ways according to the situation in which it is encountered. If a puddle of water 'disappears', the child may explain this as being because the water has drained away into the ground. If water disappears from a fish tank, children have commonly explained this in terms of the fish drinking it, flies drinking it (if it is open) or even people taking water out when no one is looking! If washing is hung on a line, the explanation is often that the water drips down.

The teacher's task is to try to enable the child to see these as related phenomena, all explained in the same way. To do this it is first necessary for the child to test out existing ideas and become convinced that they don't really fit the facts. The puddle can be lined with plastic so that water cannot seep through, the fish tank can be replaced by a tank without fish, or whatever the suggestion is, and there can be some way of catching drips from the washing. In the latter case, the washing is still wet after it stops dripping – so where does the rest of the water go? Since the washing is surrounded by air, this is the most likely situation in which the child might realize that the water 'disappears' into the air. Then the teacher can suggest that this explanation might account for the other cases where water 'disappears' and the child can think out and test out this idea against other possibilities which might have occurred.

In schematic form, the separate ideas have been brought together to form ideas which are 'bigger' in that they can be applied to a greater range of phenomena. This process continues on throughout life.

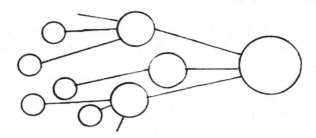

IDEAS BECOMING GRADUALLY MORE ABSTRACT

This feature is a concomitant of ideas becoming more widely applicable, since if ideas apply to many different situations they have to be independent of particular circumstances and thus related more to general aspects and less to concrete aspects. Take, for example, the case of children who explain the drops on the outside of the cold can brought into a warm room as the metal 'sweating'. The exploration of this event might involve children in finding out whether the drops appear on other surfaces in similar circumstances: on drinking glasses, on plastic containers and on other objects, such as fruit, taken out of a 'fridge'. The children will probably begin to doubt that all these things 'sweat', but even if they do not, the circumstances in which 'sweating' occurs can be investigated. A prediction made on the basis of the sweating hypothesis would lead to the expectation that, if the can were covered in plastic and brought from the fridge to the warm room, the metal should still have drops on it, because these come from the metal itself, according to this idea. The test of this prediction in practice would show drops only on the plastic and not on the tin. Since the plastic and not the metal is in contact with the air, a better explanation might begin to emerge and the role of the air (and of water vapour in it) can then be tested.

How the children come to realize that the air is the source of the drops may be via various routes, each individual (see page 77). The point relevant here is that moving to the more satisfactory idea and the one which explains all the situations where drops appear (on windows, on mirrors, etc.) means giving up the idea of the visible material being the source of the drops and being able to think in terms of the abstract idea of water being in the air in a form which cannot be seen. Not surprisingly, young children have difficulty in thinking in this way, even if they do investigate the circumstances in which the drops appear; sometimes just beginning to think that it is 'something to do with the air' is sufficient. Later, this idea can be developed further.

Most of the powerful ideas of science are abstract and many tax even adult brains when it is necessary to think in terms which do not correspond with reality (envisaging four-dimensional space, for example). But at the same time all concepts are to some extent abstract and so there is a continuum. We can begin, in the primary-school years, to help children use simple abstract ideas, but we should not expect them to be able to use more complex abstract models, such as the theory of the molecular nature of matter.

IDEAS BECOMING GRADUALLY MORE COMPLEX

The early ideas of children explain things in terms of the presence of certain parts or features. (The drum makes a sound when you bang it.) These ideas do not involve any kind of mechanism – things just happen because the parts are there; the bicycle wheels go round because of the chain, the ball comes down to earth again after being thrown up because it is heavy. Later the ideas are elaborated to indicate mechanisms and only then do they really constitute explanations. The drum makes a sound when it vibrates; the chain of the bicycle moves round with the pedal and moves the wheel it is attached to; there is the force of gravity pulling the ball down to the ground.

Each of these more advanced ideas is more complex than the previous one. This increase in complexity is a feature of more sophisticated ideas and goes on throughout the development of concepts in secondary-school education and beyond. Take the notion of 'dissolving' as an example. At first this is simply 'explained' in terms of a substance, such as sugar, having disappeared in water. Soon the child will find this too simple, because the sugar is still there (it can be tasted), and so the notion of dissolving has to take account of the fact that the sugar is still there. Then widening experience shows that it is not a matter of things dissolving or not dissolving – some things dissolve but colour the water, others dissolve partly and for everything there comes a time when no more can be dissolved. Then the idea has to be elaborated further, so that the relationship between the thing dissolving and the thing dissolving it is taken into account. To explain this relationship there has to be some explanation of what actually happens to the sugar when is goes into the water and for this it is necessary to have access to the idea of molecules of different kinds. This is far beyond the primary-school level and indeed is only really useful to those specializing in science; for others a less complex idea of dissolving is quite adequate. It shows, however, that there is always room for further elaboration of ideas in order to operate effectively at different levels.

IDEAS BECOMING GRADUALLY MORE PRECISE AND QUANTITATIVE

This is most easily seen in the way in which relationships are described. Even young children can develop some idea, for example, of the relationship between how much you 'squeeze' air and how much space it takes up. It takes more force to squeeze more air into a bicycle tyre when it is already nearly full; if you squeeze air in a potato pop-gun it is easy to see that the more force is needed the more the air is pressed into a smaller space and the more force is exerted when the potato pellet pops out. At this stage, though, the relationship is in terms of 'more pressure means less volume'. It is only much later, beyond primary school, that this relationship may be refined into the idea that there is a proportionality between the reduction in volume and the increase in pressure (which eventually will be expressed quantitatively in the gas laws).

Although children may not go beyond a qualitative relationship in primary school, the progression to more precise ideas can be helped by encouraging them to think not just about how one thing changes with another, but how much it changes. This brings us to the point of considering the role of the teacher in helping children along these directions of progress.

Ways of helping children to develop their science concepts

Some indication of how children can be helped to advance their ideas emerge from the examples given above, but it is useful to identify some strategies more explicitly. The first step in any of these is to find out about the children's ideas and for this the suggestions made in Chapter 11 will be useful.

Once the ideas have been expressed in some way, through talking, drawing, writing or indeed through action, then some useful strategies for promoting change are:
- helping children to test out their ideas;
- challenging them to use their ideas in applying them to new situation-solving problems;
- discussion so that children become aware of others' ideas and to create an opportunity to develop the language used by the children;
- asking children to represent their ideas in appropriate ways;
- encouraging children to generalize their ideas with caution.

CHILDREN TESTING OUT IDEAS

Children will cling to their ideas, which seem to make sense to them, until they are convinced that there is evidence to require some change. Often verbal reasoning and apparently logical argument have little influence; it is important for the children to see for themselves. Thus testing their ideas in practice is potentially an important means of making progress. Some examples have already been given – in testing the idea of how a puddle disappears or whether

a metal really does 'sweat'. Putting this strategy into operation depends on the teacher in several crucial ways. After finding out the child's idea, the teacher has to:
- first, take the child's idea seriously:
- second, help the child turn the idea into a form to that it can be tested;
- third, help the child do it in a way which is 'fair' so that the result is really a test of the idea (this means applying the suggestion made in the last chapter);
- fourth, help the child to interpret the results in order to establish the best explanation.

USING IDEAS AND SOLVING PROBLEMS

Without challenging their ideas directly, children can be helped to reconsider their ideas by having to use them to solve problems. Problems such as the following will require ideas to be applied and, if the initial idea does not help, then the children are likely to want to try another idea, assuming sufficient motivation:

1. Given three unbroken eggs (one of which is hard boiled, one soft boiled and one uncooked), find out which is which without breaking the eggs.
2. Given two bulbs, one battery and some wires, make the two bulbs light up as brightly as one does alone.
3. Separate sand and salt from a mixture of the two.
4. Find out which of some differently shaped containers holds the most water.
5. Find out which fertilizer is best for helping corn to grow.
6. See if you can make the cut flowers in the classroom last longer before they fade.

Some care is needed in using the problem-solving approach because its effectiveness depends on the children being motivated to solve the problem. This is most likely when they have found the problem for themselves, but it is rarely possible to arrange this at the appropriate time. Thus the timing and presentation of problems requires thought. It is best when they arise naturally out of the topic being studied, or can be fitted into it, as this provides the context and purpose for engaging with the problem. Used sparingly, problems such as those above can be fun and help progress, but over-use defeats their purpose.

DISCUSSION AND THE DEVELOPMENT OF LANGUAGE

While first-hand experience is essential to testing ideas, this does not deny that ideas can be acquired and modifications considered as a result of interaction with others – either in direct discussion or through reading or looking at pictures. The act of presenting ideas to others requires that we put them in some order, articulate aspects which may only be vaguely formed in our minds and justify the statements we make. These experiences therefore encourage children to reflect on and justify their ideas. In discussion they also realize that others have different ideas which may cause them to review their own or to challenge an opposing view.

There is much more to say about the role of language – both written and spoken – in children's learning in science, and thus a separate chapter is given over to it. The point to emphasize in this context is that the discussion during an activity and the reporting at the end of it are important means of helping children to develop their ideas, not just their communication skills.

CHILDREN REPRESENTING THEIR IDEAS

Ideas can be communicated in ways other than words and the struggle to represent an idea in a drawing or model can be as helpful in forcing reflection as a discussion with others. The way in which this seven-year-old child has chosen to represent the beating of a drum, for example, says a great deal about the way she envisages sound spreading out and dying away further from the drum, probably more than could be put into words.

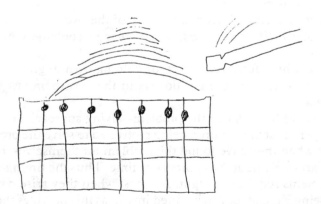

The product is useful to the teacher as an indication of the child's ideas (of which more is said in Chapter 11) but there is also value to the child in the process of representation. Deciding how to show what is meant by words forces detailed thought about what they mean. Many words, for example, are used metaphorically by adults but taken literally by children. This was revealed in one child's drawing of how the sun influences the evaporation of water – described by the child as the sun 'sucking up the water from the sea' and represented as the sun sucking on a giant drinking straw reaching down from the sky to the sea.

CHILDREN'S GENERALIZATIONS

Attempting to make generalizations is part of developing ideas into broader, more widely applicable ones. It is also essential if children are to develop – from the necessarily limited and specific activities they encounter – ideas which will help them understand a much wider range of phenomena.

Children do not need much encouragement to generalize, however. Their tendency is to do this too readily and to be over-inclusive. Claims such as 'all wood floats', 'a magnet picks up all metals' and 'electricity is dangerous' are quite often made on the basis of very limited instances. This happens in other parts of children's lives and is part of the general characteristic which leads children to assume that all dogs live in kennels (if theirs does) and to coin words such as 'bringed' instead of 'brought' by generalizing rules about language.

Without this ability to generalize, though, children would need to learn many specific instances, so it is not to be discouraged. In science, however, the reference to evidence is important and so children should be challenged to give the evidence for their generalizations and helped to be cautious about statements for which they have only limited evidence. An added benefit from this is also that it will develop the habit of regarding all general statements or principles as 'true as far as we know' but subject to revision in the light of further evidence. This lays a foundation for recognizing scientific ideas as tentative.

Chapter 7

Language, communication and reporting

Introduction

Practical activity, so essential to learning science, gains much of its value when it is the basis for talking and writing. Through using language, children have the opportunity to go back in their minds over what they have done and represent it to themselves as well as to others. It is the basis for reflection, for interpretation, for bringing experiences together so that ideas and events are linked up, and the development of concepts, as discussed in Chapter 6, becomes possible.

Many science lessons, however, are conducted in a way which denies these points. Children work in silence or murmur quietly – they are certainly not allowed to engage in challenging discussion and argument about what they are doing. At the end of an activity or a demonstration they write a formal account, following a series of headings which generally confuse and often torment them.

To change these situations, which we believe to be non-learning at best and probably of negative value in learning real science, it is necessary for teachers to be convinced of the value of talk and of less formal writing. In this chapter, therefore, we begin by discussing the role of talk in learning. We then go on to consider the problem of introducing scientific vocabulary. This is a difficult issue because, for learning with understanding, the words children use must have meaning for them; however, for good communication and the development of rigour in thinking, specialized words or specialized meanings for words are necessary.

Yet, if children do use these words, how can we be sure that they have understood what they mean?

In the third section of the chapter we consider communication through reading and writing in the context of science. Particular attention is paid to the way in which children can be encouraged to keep records and make reports which have value for them and help in their learning.

Talk and thought

Here is a conversation between a child (J) and her teacher (T) about birthdays and growing old. As you read it notice how J is sorting out ideas in her mind:

J: It's P's birthday today. He's 8 like me, but I'll be 9 next month.

T: Does it take you a whole year to get older?

J: Yes . . . no, it doesn't.

T: Are you any older today than you were yesterday?

J: No – I was 8 yesterday and I'm 8 today.

T: So now that P is 8 is he exactly the same age as you?

J: Yes.

T: If I have something to give to the one who is older who would get it?

J: P.

T: Why?

J: No, I think it would be me, because I was 8 . . . if he caught up with me I would have been it before him and he would only just have caught up.

T: Catching up – would that not make you the same age?

J: No, I don't think so. I'm older, because I'm 8 and a half.

T: Are you getting older now – tomorrow will you not be older than you are today?

J: No, I'll be the same until April the 28th.

T: What does older mean?

J: If I'm 8 and I have my birthday today and become 9 it means that . . . um . . . getting older means that when you have a birthday you get older and older each year. I'm not quite sure what old means . . . it means you get grey hair and wrinkles – I think so. It's a pattern, there's a pattern because you get smaller and then taller and then taller and then you get – big.

T: Do you carry on growing taller as you get older?

J: Yes, you do.

T: Always?

J: Sometimes you do and sometimes you don't. Because when I was a little baby I was very small and now I'm quite tall.

T: What about grown-ups? Do they go on having birthdays?

J: Yes, they do.

T: Do they continue getting taller?

J: No. I don't think they do. I'm not quite sure. I think some people do, but some people don't. When you're old you can also grow smaller.

T: Do you know anyone who's grown smaller?

J: No, but I know people who've grown bigger. My Uncle's grown huge!

T: Has he stopped growing yet?

J: No, he's still carrying on growing.
T: Is he old?
J: He's in his thirties.
T: How old is old? What would you think is old?
J: It depends on the person. If it's a weak person it doesn't take very long – if it's strong and lively it's quite long.

At the beginning J contradicted herself about whether she was older than P. Later she confused being old in years with having the characteristics of old age. These may seem artificial problems caused by the ambiguity of our language; the way we use words like 'age' and 'old' with several shades of meaning. However, language always has ambiguities and learning to use it means coming to realize that the context in which words are used has to be taken into account and that words have socially agreed meanings.

Children often have difficulty with 'everyday' use of words which have special meanings in the context of scientific activity. For example, the word 'energy' is associated with feeling active and lively in everyday usage, so it is difficult to reconcile the scientific view that after a large meal we have more energy with the feeling of being sleepy and lethargic! This confusion arises because the children have not recognized the subtle difference between an 'everyday' and a 'scientific' context in using this word.

To be able to sort out ambiguity in language it is important to *use* it: to talk to others so that one's message becomes clear; to listen to how others use words in different ways; and to question and clarify meaning and adjust one's ideas in response to the feedback.

In this next conversation (also with an eight-year-old), notice how P clarifies the teacher's meaning of the word 'distance'. Perhaps she is already aware that we often use this word in relation to time, as in 'the distant past'.

(P asked to look at the teacher's watch because she thought her own was slow.)

P: Yours says 10 to, mine's not quite on the 10.
T: How many minutes will it take for the big hand to move to number 11?
P: Five on yours, but a bit more on mine 'cos it's slow.
T: What does 'slow' mean?
P: Well, it's – um – got a bit less time.
T: Does that mean the time is really less?
P: No – it's really 10 to – if yours is right – but mine isn't going round so quickly so it hasn't got so far.
T: Let's look at the big clock. Is the distance from 10 to 11 the same as it is on my watch?
P: What do you mean . . . er . . . time?
T: I mean in the actual distance the end of the hand moves.

P: Well, that's bigger on the clock, but in time it's the same.

T: So is the end of the hand on the clock moving at the same speed as the hand on my watch?

P: No. The one on the clock is moving faster 'cos it's got a bigger distance to move round.

T: Is it still the same time it takes, then?

P: Yes.

Y: So what's wrong with your watch going more slowly than mine then?

P: Yes, but yours should go more slowly than the clock but mine shouldn't go more slowly than yours.

P's well advanced ideas about speed, time and distance can be contrasted with D's who, when asked the same question about the distance between the numbers 4 and 5 on the wall clock and on the watch, agreed that it was a greater distance on the clock. Then:

T: Is it the same on both the clock and the watch?

D: Yes, the hand moves from 4 to 5 at the same speed as each other.

T: It takes the same time, but are the two hands moving at the same speed? Remember you said it's about twice as far from 4 to 5 on the clock as it is on the watch.

D: Yes, it's the same speed and the same time – it must be.

Here D's conceptual understanding of speed and time is revealed as limited and no amount of defining words is likely to make any difference at this point. D's ideas need to be challenged by experiences which don't make sense if the same time must mean the same speed. This means that for D the words must take on different meanings and these must make sense both to D and in helping communication with others. How talk can help in this is well expressed in the following passage from an ASE publication on *Language in Science*:

> We talk ourselves into our own understandings by sharing our insights and problems with others. Most of us argue to find out what we ourselves think rather than to persuade another to our point of view. During the course of argument, new slants are put on a particular idea so that it begins to grow in another direction, or perhaps to have certain aspects cut off it. The net result of this activity is a slow change in our view of the world.[1]

The study of children's talk when involved in group tasks has shown how important exchange between children is in challenging ideas. Barnes, who pioneered much of the work in this area, called this 'exploratory' talk. He

1. Association for Science Education (ASE), Language in Science Working Party, *Language in Science*, Hatfield (United Kingdom), ASE, 1980. (Study Series, No. 16.)

showed how in science tasks the idea of one child is taken up and elaborated by another, perhaps challenged by a third, which leads them back to check with the evidence from practical investigation. It is not only concepts or ideas which are challenged, either, but the way in which an investigation is carried out or a prediction made. With several minds at work, there is less chance of ideas being tested in a superficial or unfair way than there is if one person is working alone, with no one else to challenge what he or she does. Language is the means whereby processes and ideas are challenged and this is the basis for the argument that talking is essential to learning.

Although formal reporting and organized discussion have their role in learning, Barnes emphasized the value of talk among children when there is no adult present. In such situations, working on a common problem, children interrupt each other, hesitate, and rephrase and finish each others' sentences. Ideas are thrown in without any fear of ridicule or worry that they must be wrong. As Barnes put it:

> The teacher's absence removes from their work the usual source of authority; they cannot turn to him to solve dilemmas. Thus . . . the children not only formulate hypotheses, but are compelled to evaluate them for themselves. This they can do in only two ways; by testing them against their existing view of 'how things go in the world', and by going back to the 'evidence'.[1]

That there are positive advantages of a teacher *not* being present in every group during an investigation must relieve a teacher of the guilt of not being ubiquitous. At the same time, there is a considerable burden on devising tasks which encourage this type of interaction.

Using scientific words

The right point at which to introduce and expect children to use correct 'scientific' words for the phenomena they are investigating is an issue which is bound up in the role of language in learning. General guidelines emerge from the view of learning, but the best action to take in a particular case has to be judged on the spot.

There are two main situations to consider: where children encounter an object or phenomenon for which they have no word and where children use a word inaccurately or with a very limited meaning. The first of these probably gives teachers most concern, whilst the second is actually more important and easy to overlook.

1. Douglas Barnes, *From Communication to Curriculum*, p. 29, Harmondsworth (United Kingdom), Penguin Education, 1976.

A general rule which it is useful to apply when deciding whether or not to introduce or insist on the use of a correct scientific term is to ask the following questions. Will using the correct word help the child's understanding? Does it matter if the correct word is not used? Is it important to introduce the word at this time?

The answer to these questions might be 'yes' where a distinction has to be made between one phenomenon and another: when sugar and other solids 'disappear' in water, children will use words including 'melting' to describe what has happened. It is useful to prevent confusion by introducing the word 'dissolving' and to do it *on the spot*, when examples of dissolving are in front of the children so that they know what the word labels. Another example is supplying a word to describe all the materials which allow a current to pass in a simple electric circuit. Again, having the materials and what they do in front of the children means that the word is firmly attached to at least some examples of its meaning.

In other instances, providing names can wait, or may not even be important. This may well apply when children are looking at a number of different things – perhaps a collection of minerals or what they have caught in pond dipping. Here the introduction of correct names is likely to interfere with the main purpose, that of realizing the variety of things there are, and if children want to refer to individual items they can use their own descriptive labels ('the purple crystal' or 'the wriggly thin red worm') for this purpose. Children can be told that these things do have names, which can be found in books, but that most people (including their teacher) don't know them because they don't need to use them. (There is more about naming things in the context of field studies on p. 214.)

When children have a perfectly good word – such as 'grip' for a rough surface where there is friction – the answer to the questions above might well be 'no'. Until their experience leads them to want to describe the much more abstract phenomenon of friction, the word cannot have the correct meaning for them and so would be unhelpful.

The main principle here is to provide words when they have meaning in terms of the children's experience and will be useful to them. The word should fill a perceived gap in the children's vocabulary and should be one that they need to use. In contrast words introduced without need in prior experience are likely to be forgotten immediately or used inappropriately. As children develop and their experience becomes richer, they need more words to distinguish phenomena and describe objects more accurately. Thus there will come a time when it is helpful to use the word 'respiration' rather than 'breathing', for example, but to do this before a distinction between the two is evident in experience will only confuse. It does children no service to feed them words which they cannot use because they are not sure of their meaning.

The inaccurate or limited or over-inclusive use of a word in science is a normal part of children's learning. As concepts become more widely applicable (see Chapter 6), it is inevitable that the meaning of words has to shift. So we should see the development of vocabulary as part of the development of children's understanding, not as a matter of 'giving the right word'. Children will, then, necessarily use scientific words somewhat idiosyncratically. They also pick up technical words from the media, friends and other sources out of school and attempt to use them. All this adds up to a situation where children may be using words intending a different meaning than the accepted one.

To develop better understanding, it is useful to discuss words with the children, wherever possible with some direct experience of the phenomenon available at the time. When discussing what the children mean by the word 'vibration', some objects which can vibrate should be present. Children can be asked to find other examples of what they think is 'vibrating' and opinions of others can be sought. So, if a glowing colour is produced as something which is 'vibrating', there can be a discussion which helps to clear the confusion arising from the metaphorical use of the word. This could be a good moment to introduce another word to describe the intense colour.

In summary, then, the development of children's vocabulary can be helped by:
- providing words when they are needed to describe or label something of which the children already have experience; and
- discussing words which children use to find out what they mean by them and developing this into more conventional use.

Reading and writing

Verbal communication also includes reading and writing but here there is less opportunity for the close dialogue which helps to clarify words in speech. It is important not to confuse real understanding with mere information. To consider the difference, imagine that someone has told you of the existence of things called 'keets' and you read the following passage about them:

> Keets are intriguing and useful objects because they are keetic. Some occur naturally and many are man-made. It is thought that ancient man may have used them for gathering sticks but since they rot away in most climates there is no firm evidence of this. Natural keets are made of the rare hip-wood. Some other materials can be made keetic if they are brought up to a keet in a special way; they must point towards the moon and be rubbed together in a circular movement. When two keets are brought towards each other a low-pitched note is heard which rises in pitch as they come closer together. The noise can be arrested by placing a thick piece of wood between them, so keets are always packed in wooden boxes with sep-

arate compartments for each. Keets gradually become less keetic if they are exposed to noise so it is important not to speak too loudly, and especially not to sing, when close to them. Several keets can be made into one large one which will be as loud as all the small ones separately. Keets are used in the trilling industry for tuning instruments and for measuring distances.

Can you now answer the following questions about keets:
- Do they occur naturally?
- What can they be made from?
- When do they make a noise?
- What changes the pitch of their note? etc.

You probably can, even though you have no idea what a keet is. It is useful to reflect on why you do not understand and yet can answer the factual questions.

Keets may seem too fantastic to you, but this is only because you have a wide experience of materials. We do not need to go into the realms of fantasy to consider what happens to children in circumstances where they do not have the wide experience. The following passage from the *Children's Britannica*, about lasers, illustrates the point:

> From an ordinary light source, such as a lamp bulb, light streams in all directions, just as when a stone is thrown into a pond the ripples radiate outwards in ever-widening circles, becoming fainter and fainter as they go. This kind of light is known as incoherent light, that is, it does not cohere or stick together, but spreads all around. But in the laser things may be so arranged that all the light comes out in the same direction. This kind of light is known as coherent light. If the light is concentrated like this into a very narrow beam, the source appears extremely bright. The most powerful laser sources are brighter than any others that can be made – in fact they are much brighter than the Sun.[1]

While these passages may not seem very helpful in developing understanding, there clearly is a place for books in helping children to learn about science. Apart from books which are intended to be the basis for classroom work, the purposes which books for children can serve in science include:
- expanding the range of children's experience at second hand, through illustrations and accounts of things beyond the children's immediate environment;
- setting science within a human context through accounts of the work of scientists and technologists, and stories of past and present discoveries;
- linking to other subjects by embedding science within stories, poems, etc.;

1. Robin Sales and Brian Williams (eds.), *Children's Britannica*, 3rd ed. rev., Vol. 10, p. 174, London, Encyclopaedia Britannica, 1981.

- providing further information about things they will have encountered and how things in their experience work.

Good communication through reading enables the reader to have a dialogue with the text, to question it, to be challenged by it and to make it part of one's own thinking. Similar considerations apply to children's writing; to be most useful it should be part of a dialogue between child and teacher.

Both informal and formal writing can be the basis for dialogue. Too often the only kind of written account which is considered in science is the formal report at the end of an investigation. For many children, this is a formidable task and mars the whole enjoyment of the activity. Often the only purpose children see for this report is to satisfy the teacher. The problem is that this is often a waste of time for both the child and the teacher who has to mark it. It does not help children to appreciate the value of communication in writing. For this it is best to build up the use of informal notes by children, starting with what they need to write down, since they cannot remember everything which happens in an investigation.

Allowing and encouraging children to use a personal notebook in which they put down what they want and need to record, for themselves and for no one else, is a good way of helping them use writing, not only as an *aide-mémoire* but also to sort out their ideas. Scientific activity is systematic activity and using a notebook helps in keeping observations in an orderly fashion, recalling where certain observations were made and drawing diagrams to show exactly how things were before and after certain changes were made. Children need to learn how to do this and they can only do it by having and using a notebook themselves. The teacher can help by suggesting what sorts of things might be noted down, by giving hints about putting results into a table and by showing how labels can be attached to drawings.

These notebooks should not be marked, but they can be read. They are of great value to a teacher in showing how children are thinking. The temptation for a teacher to 'correct' what is there should be resisted and instead comments can be made in writing which constitute a written dialogue with the child. This example illustrates the approach:

Maria, quietly working with her balance, chose a pile of cotton wool and a small rubber. She placed them both on her balance and was surprised that the tiny rubber was heavier than the big fluff of cotton wool. She called her teacher to come and see. He showed interest and talked to her. Maria demonstrated how she came to her unexpected conclusion: 'See? The rubber goes down and the cotton goes up.' Then the teacher asked her, 'Can you find something that is lighter than the cotton wool?' and went his way. Maria tried several objects until she found a peanut which was lighter than the cotton wool. She took her book and wrote, 'I put cotton on one side and my rubber on the other. When I put a peanut, the cotton went down.' When her teacher saw this cryptogram, he made the following comments. To the first part he added, 'What did your balance look like?' and concerning the second part he asked, 'Where did you put the peanut?'

This teacher effectively helped Maria to make her notes better without creating fear or tension. It did not take Maria long to add her drawing of the balance with the cotton up and the side with the rubber down. She also wrote, 'The rubber was heavier. Then I put a peanut instead of the rubber, and the peanut was lighter.' And this she illustrated with a fresh drawing of the balance in reverse position. And, what is more, she thought it was all her own idea.[1]

1. Jos Elstgeest, Wynne Harlen and David Symington, 'Children Communicate', in: W. Harlen (ed.), *Primary Science: Taking the Plunge* . . ., op. cit., pp. 100–1.

Chapter 8

Encouraging and handling children's questions

Introduction: the importance of asking questions

We all ask questions when we want to know something, or when we are puzzled or curious about something. Our questions show what we do not know and what we would like to know. Children's questions are no different; they give an important lead to what the children have already understood and what they have not understood. They mark the cutting edge of children's learning. Sometimes, too, in the way they are expressed, children's questions indicate their pre-conceptions (as when a young girl looked at a particularly aggressive-looking cactus plant and asked 'Is there an animal inside it?').

Thus encouraging children to ask all kinds of questions is important, for through this means they can fill in some links between one experience and another, and gain the help they need in making sense of their experience. But scientific activity can only answer certain kinds of questions, ones which ask about what there is in the world around and how it behaves. In answer to these kinds of questions assertions can be made which can be verified by investigation. Examples are 'Does wood float in water?' 'Do trees grow at the top of high mountains?' In contrast there are questions such as 'Should happiness be the aim of life?' or 'What is the nature of knowledge?' which are philosophical and not answerable by scientific inquiry. There are also questions of human motivation ('Why do martyrs sacrifice their lives?') and of aesthetic judgement ('Which of these pieces of music is most attractive?') which are quite different from the kinds of question answered by science.

Recognizing the difference between different kinds of questions is important for teachers in helping them respond to children's questions. It is also necessary so that children can be encouraged, within science activities, to pose questions which they can answer by action. This chapter attempts to give teachers help in developing the skills of encouraging certain kinds of ques-

95

tions while being capable of handling all kinds of questions which children constantly ask.

Types of question

Here are some questions which children asked when they met a marine biologist. (The age of the child involved is in brackets following each question.)

- Is it possible that there are creatures we don't know about at the bottom of the sea? (10)
- Why are crabs inside out? (8)
- How do sea urchins swim? (5)
- How do you become a marine biologist? (11)
- Why is the sea salty? (6)
- How old is the oldest fish? (9)
- Why do fishes live under water? (6)
- What is the average age that fish live to? (11)
- Why do some sharks eat people and some don't? (9)

These are the sorts of questions children ask about a subject they are interested in; the sort which are very difficult even for an expert to answer and in some cases impossible to answer in a way which could be understood by children of the age who asked them.

This may or may not be comforting to the primary-school teacher, who is not a marine expert and yet is the one who will be asked similar questions on this and every other subject by the children!

It also may or may not be comforting to know that it is quite often *not* the best thing to do to attempt to answer the child's question, because:
- children can be deterred from questioning if they receive answers which they cannot understand;
- a question is not always what it seems (in other words, it does not always require an answer); and
- giving the answer may prevent children from finding it out and learning something in their own terms.

Instead of thinking that every question has to be answered, it is best to study questions and learn how to *handle* them, not necessarily to *answer* them.

We can categorize most of children's questions into five types:
1. Questions which are not asked for information but are really comments expressed as questions ('Why are birds so clever that they can weave nests with their beaks?').
2. Questions requiring simple factual answers which can be readily understood by the child ('Where was this bird's nest found?').
3. Questions which would require complex answers which the child would

be unlikely to understand ('Why do some birds build nests and others don't?').

4. Questions which could readily be answered by the child through investigation or inquiry ('What is the nest made of?').

5. Philosophical questions ('Do birds enjoy making their nests?').

As an exercise try categorizing each of the questions to the marine biologist. (Note that some questions might be capable of simple answers but still be ones which children could investigate for themselves. These should be categorized as (4).)

Do this first by yourself and then, if there is an opportunity, discuss your results with others and try to reconcile any differences.

Questions in category (4) are the most productive for science activities and the ones we should encourage children to ask. This can be done by example, when teachers ask questions which encourage scientific activity. It is worth practising this skill and the following exercise is designed to do this.

TEACHERS' QUESTIONS WHICH ENCOURAGE ACTIVE LEARNING

Imagine that a child comes up to you, his or her teacher, and proudly shows you a leaf that he or she finds interesting and has picked up on the way to school. What questions about the leaf can you ask the child that will start him or her investigating scientifically? (Such questions may not be the first response to the child but they are appropriate at some point and so need to be thought out.)

Information questions	*Action questions*
Promote science as information.	Promote science as a way of working.
Answers derived from secondary sources by talking/reading.	Answers derived from first-hand experience involving practical action materials.
Tend to emphasize answering as the achievement of a correct end-product (the right answers).	Encourage awareness that varied answers may each be 'correct' in their own terms and view achievement as what is learned in the process of arriving at an answer.
Successful answering is most readily achieved by verbally fluent children who have confidence and facility with words.	Successful answering is achievable by all children.

Write down your questions. Share them with others and then decide whether they really meet the criteria of *action* questions – that is (a) they stimulate answer-seeking through active investigation and they encourage children to use their own ideas and communicate the fact that these ideas are valued – or whether (b) they are asking the child for information.

The educational significance of the distinction can be seen from the summary of their implications given in the table on page 97.

QUESTIONS THAT ENCOURAGE CHILDREN TO USE
SPECIFIC SCIENTIFIC SKILLS

We can extend the notion of phrasing questions to promote active investigation to target particular process skills. This is useful when a teacher is aware that certain children will benefit from, say, being required to make more detailed observations or trying to plan a fair test.

The approach can most easily be conveyed through an example. Suppose children are undertaking to study the germination of seeds. They begin by looking at a collection of dry seeds before planting them. Then they prepare for planting seeds in various conditions and in various ways which test some of their ideas or might answer their questions (such as 'Will the seeds grow just as well upside down?'). They plant some seeds in different conditions which they help to decide. They observe, measure and discuss the growth over a period of time and make some interpretation of the results which leads to more questions and more trials.

At various points in these activities, the teacher could ask questions such as those below which would lead children to use and refine their process skills whilst developing their experience of seeds and ideas about growth.

To encourage children to observe
- What are the differences between these seeds (of different types)?
- What are the differences between these seeds (of the same type)?
- What is the same about these different types of seed?
- What are the differences in the plants from different seeds?
- What is the same about plants from different seeds?

To encourage children to raise questions
- What would you like to know about these seeds?
- What would you like to find out about these plants?

To encourage children to hypothesize
- Why do you think these (dry) seeds are not growing?
- What do you think will make them grow?
- Why do you think some seeds are growing more quickly than others?

- How do you think we could make them grow more quickly?

To encourage children to devise and plan investigations
- What will you need to do to try out your ideas about what will make the seeds grow (or the plants grow better)?
- What equipment will you need?
- What is the thing to do first . . . and then . . . and then?
- How will you make sure that it is a *fair* test?
- What will you look for to find out the result?

To encourage children to measure and calculate
- How many seeds of each kind are growing?
- How much are they growing each day/each week?
- How does the growth vary from day to day/week to week?

To encourage children to find patterns and relationships
- Was there any connection between the size of the seed and how quickly it grew?
- What difference did the amount of water (or sun, or the type of soil) make to the way the seed grew?

To encourage children to make predictions (when the seeds are growing and relationships have been found)
- What do you think will happen if we give the seedlings more (or less) water?
- How much do you think they will grow if we double (or halve) the amount of water?

To encourage children to design and make
- Can you make a device that will water the seeds evenly and regularly?
- How could we weigh the seeds whilst they are growing?

To encourage children to reflect critically
- In what way could you improve your investigation if you started again?
- Can you think of a different and better way of trying out your ideas?

To encourage children to communicate
- How can you explain to others what you have done and found out?
- What is the best way to keep a record of the way the seeds grew?

Handling children's questions

Although we may encourage children to ask action or investigable questions, they will always ask all kinds of questions and these have to be addressed in some way. By emphasizing the value of action questions we do not imply that only these type need be heeded. To dismiss any of the children's questions risks deterring further questions and thereby losing a valuable source of information for helping their learning.

The following passages by Jelly from *Primary Science: Taking the Plunge*[1] describe a strategy for turning questions which may not at first appear to be action questions into ones which can start children investigating. It is particularly useful for those questions, categorized as (3) above which could only be answered in terms of concepts beyond the grasp of primary-school children.

> Spontaneous questions from children come in various forms and carry a variety of meanings. Consider, for example, the following questions. How would you respond to each?
>
> 1. What is a baby tiger called?
> 2. What makes it rain?
> 3. Why can you see yourself in a window?
> 4. Why is the hamster ill?
> 5. If I mix these (paints), what colour will I get?
> 6. If God made the world, who made God?
> 7. How long do cows live?
> 8. How does a computer work?
> 9. When will the tadpoles be frogs?
> 10. Are there people in outer space?
>
> Clearly the nature of each question shapes our response to it. Even assuming we wanted to give children the correct answers, we could not do so in all cases. Question 6 has no answer, but we can of course respond to it. Question 10 is similar; it has no certain answer but we could provide a conjectural one based on some relevant evidence. All the other questions do have answers, but this does not mean that each answer is similar in kind, nor does it mean that all answers are known to the teacher, nor are all answers equally accessible to children. . . .
>
> Not only do questions vary in kind, requiring answers that differ in kind, but children also have different reasons for asking a question. The question may mean 'I want a direct answer', it might mean 'I've asked the question to show you I'm interested but I'm not after a literal answer', or it could mean 'I've asked the question because I want your attention – the answer is not important'. Given all these variables how then should we handle the questions raised spontaneously in science work? . . .

1. Sheila Jelly, 'Helping Children Raise Questions – and Answering Them', in: W. Harlen (ed.), *Primary Science: Taking the Plunge . . .*, op. cit., pp. 53–5.

What follows is a suggested strategy . . . It's not the only strategy possible, nor is it completely infallible, but it has helped a large number of teachers deal with difficult questions. By difficult questions I mean those that require complex information and/or explanation for a full answer. The approach does not apply to simple informational questions such as 1, 7 and 9 on the list above because these are easy to handle, either by telling or by reference to books, or expertise, in ways familiar to the children in other subject areas . . . Essentially it is a strategy for handling complex questions and in particular those of the 'why' kind that are the most frequent of all spontaneous questions.

The strategy recommended is one that turns the question to practical action with a 'let's see what we can do to understand more' approach. The teaching skill involved is the ability to 'turn' the question. Consider, for example, a situation in which children are exploring the properties of fabrics. They have dropped water on different types and become fascinated by the fact that water stays 'like a little ball' on felt. They tilt the felt, rolling the ball around, and someone asks 'Why is it like a ball?' How might the question be turned by applying the 'doing more to understand' approach? We need to analyse the situation quickly and use what I call a 'variables scan'.

The explanation must relate to something 'going on' between the water and the felt surface so causing the ball. That being so, ideas for children's activities will come if we consider ways in which the situation could be varied to better understand the making of the ball. We could explore surfaces keeping the drop the same, and explore drops keeping the surface the same. These thoughts can prompt others that bring ideas nearer to what children might do.

For example:
1. *Focusing on the surface, keeping the drop the same:*
   - What is special about the felt that helps make the ball?
   - Which fabrics are good 'ball-makers'?
   - Which are poor?
   - What have the good ball-making fabrics in common?
   - What surfaces are good ball-makers?
   - What properties do these share with the good ball-making fabrics?
   - Can we turn the felt into a poor ball-maker?
2. *Focusing on the water drop, keeping the surface the same:*
   - Are all fluids good ball-makers?
   - Can we turn the water into a poor ball-maker?

Notice how the 'variables scan' results in the development of productive questions that can be explored by the children. The original question has been turned to practical activity and children exploring along these lines will certainly enlarge their understanding of what is involved in the phenomenon. They will not arrive at a detailed explanation but may be led towards simple generalization of their experience, such as 'A ball will form when . . .' or 'It will not form when . . .'.

Some teachers . . . are uneasy that the original question remains unanswered, but does this matter? The question has promoted worthwhile scientific inquiry and we must remember that its meaning for the child may well have been 'I'm asking it to communicate my interest'. For such children interest has certainly been developed and children who may have initiated the question as a request for explanation in practice, are normally satisfied by the work their question generates.

The strategy can be summarized as follows:

Analyse the question
↓
Consider if it can be 'turned' to practical activity
(with its 'real' materials or by simulating them)
↓
Carry out a 'variables scan' and identify productive questions
↓
Use questions to promote activity
↓
Consider simple generalizations children might make *from experience.*

Chapter 9

Science outside the classroom

Introduction

The environment of every school is a ready-made source of objects, happenings and relationships to investigate. Thus even if a school has few internal resources for active science, it is never short of an environment which can support a great deal of scientifically and educationally valuable activity. Not only are almost all the materials to use outside the classroom free but they also have an intrinsic reality. Ideas developed through their study do not afterwards have to be applied to 'real' life, as do many classroom activities, for they are found in the real situation and immediately help in understanding it.

This chapter has two sections, both of which include activities for teachers relating to preparing activities for children. In the first section we describe a way of using the environment to stimulate curiosity, to encourage careful observation and to bring about an awareness that one can learn from and about everything in the surrounding environment. The technique is one of devising a 'trail' which children can follow from 'station' to 'station' where they undertake tasks which involve some mental and physical activity, and lead to enhanced appreciation of their immediate environment. A trail can be set up in any environment, built or natural; indeed it can be restricted to the school buildings themselves if need be. The activities at the stations are brief and necessarily superficial, but they can be the start of further inquiries.

The second section deals with deeper and more sustained investigation of parts of the natural environment requiring access to ground in which plants grow and small creatures live. A garden or park can supply these if access to more natural vegetation is difficult. The extended and ordered study of a particular plot of ground gives the opportunity for relationships to be seen between different things living together and the effect on these of the physical conditions of the soil, the weather and the presence or absence of shelter, shade or sun. Such studies provide opportunities to connect related findings into more widely applicable concepts.

An activity trail

An activity trail is designed to lead people (teachers or children) to a number of places (called 'stations') in the immediate surroundings. At each station they are presented with some challenge. The stations can be indicated by numbers on a rough map or people can be led to them by brief route instructions. The challenge at each station is presented in the form of a question in a few words on a paper drawn up beforehand by the 'trail makers'. The answer to the question must be obtainable by some activity carried out on the spot—most commonly by careful observation, but sometimes by reasoning, measurement, estimation or a simple experiment, and in many cases, by discussion.

An activity trail can be set up in *any* environment. It can be just an interesting in 'concrete jungle' as in a garden. There is no environment which cannot provide the setting for a trail. Of course every environment and trail is unique and so we cannot provide an example that anyone can take away and use. However we can give some examples of 'stations' which have been used and which can be adapted to suit particular situations. Some of these clearly use built structures and others natural features of the environment.

EXAMPLES OF 'STATIONS' IN AN ACTIVITY TRAIL

1. Stand outside the door on the steps.
   Make five different observations which indicate that a wind is blowing. Estimate the wind strength.
2. Choose any car in the car park. Look at it carefully for signs which tell you something about its history. Does it tell you anything about its owner?
3. Stand half-way along the path to the gate. Note all the different sounds that you hear in 2 minutes.
   Sort your sounds into two groups. In how many different ways can you do this?
   Select a frequent loud sound. Find out how far away you have to walk before you can no longer hear it.
4. Find the large 'flame of the forest' tree behind the playground.
   Estimate the height of the tree.
5. Look at the stones in the wall at the back of the flower bed. Do you think they are just decorative or a structural part of the wall? Give your reasons.
6. Notice the direction of the flower heads of the sunflowers. Can you account for the way they are facing?

7. Wet your hand in the pond and make a wet print on the ground.
   How long do you think it will take to dry? Find out. Find a way to make it
   dry faster.

8. Look at the roof of the garden shelter.
   Estimate how many tiles it has.

9. Look out across all the land from the building to the hills in the distance.
   What evidence is there of human presence more than 50 years ago?
   What evidence of human presence between 10 years and 20 years ago?
   What evidence is there of human presence in the last year?
   What evidence is there of human presence in the last week?

10. Look at the two bushes of the same kind growing on either side of the
    path.
    What differences do you notice in how they are growing?
    Propose three alternative reasons for these differences.

PRINCIPLES IN MAKING AN ACTIVITY TRAIL

Some general points can readily be drawn together from these examples which
guide the making of a trail:

1. The questions asked are 'action' questions not factual ones (see page 97).
2. The challenges draw the participants into more careful use of their senses,
   into making comparisons, postulating hypotheses, seeking evidence – in
   other words, using process skills.
3. The stations can be created in one of two main ways: either by looking at a
   particularly interesting or unusual feature of the environment and posing
   an action question about it or by starting from a particular activity (such as
   estimating or pattern finding) and finding a situation which lends itself to
   being a subject for this activity (any tree's height, or the number of leaves
   it has, could be estimated).
4. The stations of the trail should be independent of each other so that people can start at any station and need not visit them in any order.
5. People should work in groups (of three or four) and carry out the activities
   as a group; the station activities should, where possible, take advantage of
   the group and encourage discussion.

PURPOSES OF A TRAIL

As we said in the introduction, a trail is not intended to be a thorough study of
the environment. It serves quite different but equally valuable purposes, particularly in the context of a teachers' course.

First, working on a trail is a good 'ice-breaker'; it gets people talking and
working together, and it helps them to get to know the surroundings if these

are not familiar. Second, it provides experiences of carrying out process skills which can be later discussed. Finally, it uses no equipment and yet it enables information to be gained through scientific activity. All of these purposes are best served by setting up a trail as an early activity (the first, perhaps, after formalities have been completed) in a teachers' course.

Later the use of a trail with children can be discussed. It is probably quite evident from the examples that stations can be the starting points for extended activity on a particular topic (evaporation, for example, or the conditions which favour healthy growth of plants).

Scientific study of the living environment

The environment of the school is as rich a source of scientific information as any textbook. Like a book, however, it is necessary to know how to read it before it can add to our learning. Children need to learn how to study this 'book', particularly as, being so familiar to them as part of their daily experience, it is easy for the features of the environment to be taken for granted. But to help the children, teachers also need to know how to read the 'book of the school environment'. It will be necessary for the teacher to make a biological and ecological survey of the school's immediate surroundings so as to recognize and assess its potential for children's scientific activity.

Preparations for working with children in the field, over and above planning the logistics of reaching the area for study and deciding how to ensure orderly behaviour, must involve: preparing questions which stimulate the children to formulate questions to investigate and to take up the problems which are to be found in this part of the living environment; thinking out how to guide the children to find answers to these problems and questions, that is, to practise and develop process skills; and planning ways to help the children to organize their observations and learning so that instead of being content with isolated findings, they seek to connect the ideas they form into relationships and conceptual patterns of understanding. When teacher and children discuss their work (what they say, what they did, why they did it, and what they observed and concluded), relationships of cause and effect, of dominance of one thing over another, of physical influence, of parental care, of interference, etc., can be pointed out.

AN EXAMPLE: PREPARING FOR WORK ON A 'MINIFIELD'

A minifield is a piece of ground which is chosen because it looks interesting for some reason or other, and is marked out using string, sticks or a hoop. It is usually about one square metre in area (see Part Two, page 201).

To identify what preparation is needed by a teacher, let us first anticipate what children will be doing when working on their minifield. They will probably find a variety of plants in different stages of growth, and of varying size and appearance. They can count the number of individual plants of the same kind and the number of different kinds that are found. They can map the topographical position of plants of the same kind within the minifield and so record spatial relationships among the plants and other features. They can find which plant dominates, either by occurring most, or by its size. By then they will already have started to establish certain relationships, either spontaneously or with prompting from their teacher. A question as to whether the dominating plant seems to have an influence on the others can start the children looking for a different type of relationship, such as might explain why a patch of ground (perhaps under the spreading flat leaves of a common dandelion in a lawn) is bare.

If the children are to develop the skills and attitudes for noticing and investigating these sorts of occurrences and develop the habit of using observations and predictions to develop understanding, then they need the encouragement of their teacher. This can take the form of things being pointed out or a question which sets them reasoning. The best preparation for this role is for the teacher to have experienced personally the exploration of similar minifields and to have discussed the significance of what they have done and found with others. Thus the activities to be found under the title 'Children and their Environment' (Chapter 15) should be undertaken by teachers in the first place. Teachers who have never done such activities before should do them a number of times in different situations.

Once familiar with the general possibilities of minifields, the particular patches of ground to be studied at a particular time must be surveyed before children are taken to work on them. This enables the teacher to think of appropriate questions and problems for the children to undertake.

Studies of minifields by teachers, during in-service or pre-service courses, have a twofold benefit. The teachers can approach the study at their own level, since challenges exist at any level of intellectual engagement when investigations begin. At the same time, they can consider how children might engage with the minifield and how the various points of interest might be brought to the attention of the children. Activities at both these levels have added value when discussed with others. Questions such as the following might form the agenda for a critical review of this experience.

About the educational value of studying a minifield

What science process skills can be practised in this study? What did you learn yourself in terms of skills and concepts and what might children learn? What additional investigable questions can be raised from the observations? Does the record made (map or description of findings) adequately represent what was done and found? Was there sufficient evidence on which to base a reliable conclusion? Was there sufficient challenge and interest to motivate activity to answer questions? Is such a detailed study of a minifield capable of leading to the grasp of the complexities of a community of living things? Does focusing on a minifield distract from a more comprehensive view of an area or give significance to features which might otherwise be missed?

About the organization of studying a minifield

Did you have everything you needed? In what way was it best to define the boundary of the minifield and what would be the best size? Was the time allocated for the activity sufficient? How long might children sustain work on the area? What instructions beforehand would be necessary? What information beforehand would be helpful?

About follow-up work

What can be done with the information obtained? How suitable is mapping the area as a means of recording findings? What can be done with the records – would it be useful to put them together to represent a larger area or to make comparisons between one area and another?

Personal experience of the challenge of investigation and of the subsequent discussion helps teachers to gain confidence in planning learning activities for children. The activities can also be more carefully targeted for different groups of children. The youngest children (up to 7 or 8) might for example best take a hoop to define their areas, throwing it down almost anywhere and then counting the flowers caught in its area. They might be asked whether all the flowers look the same. The question then turns to how many different kinds there are, leading the children to look more closely at the distinguishing features of plants. In doing so they will find small creatures crawling underneath, making the whole place one of interest and discovery.

Small children have difficulty confining their attention to the area within their hoop, but this does not matter because the purpose is for the children to observe carefully, to distinguish between living things and to begin to realize the variety of living things in even a small area.

Older children can be more systematic, listing what they find in their minifield and finding which is the most frequently occurring and how this one seems to dominate. This is an introduction to the study of a community where concepts of competition, dominance and interdependence can be formed.

Useful extensions of minifield work include establishing some characteristics of a particular woodland or of a meadow, or a moor, and finding out how seasonal differences influence a particular area, which may be represented by one or more minifields. In respect to the former, data from a number of mini-fields studied by different groups within these areas can be combined to reveal the general and common characteristics. This adds importance to accurate description, mapping and the collection of samples. As for the latter extension, the observations need to be made in the same minifields at different times of the year and the records have to be accurate enough for reliable comparisons to be made later. Children will then learn not only about the seasonal changes but also the skills of accurate observation and recording.

More work in the living environment

The principles of what has been discussed for working with minifields apply equally to other activities described in 'Children and their Environment'. Using basically the same techniques, these other activities lead to more com-prehensive results and more widely applicable concepts and generalizations.

In the exercise 'A Biofield in Layers' (page 205) several groups choose the same area for study but each group confines itself to a definite layer or level above (and if appropriate) below the ground.

'Working on a Transect' (page 206) takes a step beyond the close com-munity of living things in a minifield. A transect cuts a narrow path across a larger area. It is usually marked out by string between two points which are anything from 2 to 5 metres apart. It is most interesting if the transect cuts across one or more transitions in the vegetation. The idea is to investigate a narrow strip of ground, some 20 cm wide along the string, rather as if it were a long, narrow minifield. Because of its shape there is more variation along it and the changes in vegetation can often be related to visible conditions such as the composition of the soil, the exposure to wind or sunshine, the slope of the land, or the influence of humans in passing over it or cultivating it.

The concepts of 'vegetation' and 'flora and fauna' are rather abstract and begin to have meaning through a number of experiences in the field. Vegeta-tion is more than the plant cover of an area. It gives the landscape (or elements of a landscape such as an embankment, the verge of a lane or the edge of a pond) its own colour and character. It is influenced by the prevailing physical conditions and by the activities of creatures living in it. Studying a transect in relation to certain questions which lead children to think about the things which are there and which influence them will help children towards the more abstract concepts. Examples of such questions are given on pages 208 and 209 but every transect will call for its own specific questions. It is a good idea to practise adapting these questions to suit the particular area being stu-died during a preparatory survey of the ground.

Questions used in field-work are of a special nature: they do not call for immediate answers; they call for a response which is in terms of doing – looking, probing, comparing and thinking (cf. action questions, page 97). What will be expressed in words as 'answers' depends entirely on the quality of the actions. Most likely questions, even if they are answered by doing something, also act as triggers for more questions, either in the field or later when the work is continued in the classroom (see pages 100–2).

NAMING NAMES

Teachers may fear undertaking field studies because they realize that they are not familiar with the names of the plants and animals which will be encountered. It is a mistake to think that knowing names is a requirement for studying living things. Nothing could be less true for it is no handicap in handling real living things.

Two points may help. First, one's own everyday knowledge need not be underestimated; it may be based on popular knowledge, unscientific and patchy, but it is a start. It enables one to distinguish between trees, shrubs and weeds. Everybody readily recognizes almost all species belonging to the largest plant family – grass. Many are familiar with the common local names given to plants and animals which are found in a particular spot. Second, adding a descriptive adjective to a well-known general name works wonders in helping communication.

One can observe what things are like, how they behave towards one another, what their distinguishing features are and how they struggle for survival in their environment, but one cannot observe their name. So knowing names is not 'knowing' the living things themselves. Nevertheless, it is worthwhile becoming familiar with the common names of the plants and animals which occur frequently in the neighbourhood. This can be done gradually, by asking people who know the names or by using an identification key or flora. Children can use certain versions of these references so that they learn the skills of 'looking things up'. Although this can be fascinating and satisfying, it must be remembered that naming plants and animals is only relevant in relation to communicating with other people, not in relation to communicating with the plant or animal itself.

Chapter 10

Assessment as part of teaching

Introduction

This chapter, the first of two on assessment, is mainly concerned with informal assessment, an essential part of teaching (Chapter 11 deals with formal assessment, tests and examinations, important because they frequently dominate the curriculum).

First, however, there are some introductory points about assessment in general and assessment in science in particular.

We begin with the following definition of assessment: 'Assessment is a process of gathering information in which the actual evidence of performance is replaced by something which signifies a judgement of it. In the process of assessment some attempt is made to apply a standard or criterion to the information.'

There are three points to make about this definition. First, it draws attention to the existence of a wide range of ways of gathering information about children's performance. Testing is just one of the possible ways, but there are many others. Thus *assessment does not mean testing; testing is just one way of carrying out assessment.* Second, in assessment the actual performance (the piece of work or what a child said or did) is replaced by something which indicates a judgement on it. This 'something' might be a mark, a comment, a grade or even a smile or a frown. Only what replaced it then exists and necessarily *some of the information in the original performance is lost.* In contrast, if the actual performance could be preserved (the piece of work, or a video recording of what children did and said) then the whole information is retained. However, we have to allow assessment to replace the actual performance for obvious practical reasons. Third, the standards or criteria used as a basis for making the judgement can be of different kinds leading to assessment which is *norm-referenced* – where the standard of judgement is what the average child can do; or *criterion-referenced* – where the judgement is in terms of whether what a child does meets certain criteria, irrespective of how others perform; or *child-referenced* – where the judgement is based on expectations of the individual child.

Child-referenced assessment enables a teacher to reward signs of progress whether or not the pupil is behind others or meets certain performance criteria. It has an important role in feedback to the pupil. However, it cannot be used where pupils are being compared with each other or where decisions are being made about where children are in progress towards common goals. Norm-referenced assessment is not the best choice in these circumstances because it does not give information about what children can or cannot do. Where this is required, criterion-referencing is most helpful.

Purposes of assessment

Children are assessed at various times for different reasons. The purposes fall into three main categories, although these can be sub-divided: (a) diagnostic (sometimes called 'formative') – for identifying problems and points of progress so that appropriate next steps may be planned; (b) summarizing achievement (summative) – for reporting formally on what pupils have achieved at certain stages of schooling (such as end of year or end of the primary phase); and (c) monitoring standards of the school – for enabling evaluation of some parts of the work of the school or of schools in a region. The first of these purposes is the subject of this chapter and the second of the next. Assessment for evaluative purposes does not affect the individual child and will not be discussed further.

The importance of assessment as part of teaching

The need to find out children's ideas, skills and attitudes follows from the view of learning which underpins this book (see Chapter 1) and which can be summed up by the old adage 'start from where the child is'. Another way of expressing the same idea is in terms of 'matching', that is, providing experiences for children which present just the right amount of challenge.

> There has to be the right mixture of the familiar and the novel, the right match to the stage of learning the child has reached. If the material is too familiar or the learning skills too easy, children will become inattentive and bored. If too great maturity is demanded of them, they fall back on half-remembered formulae and become concerned only to give the reply the teacher wants. Children can think

and form concepts, so long as they work at their own level, and are not made to feel that they are failures.[1]

Some further good reasons for 'matching' can be added to those given in this quotation. First, that theories of learning (including those of Piaget, Bruner and Ausubel) suggest that if a new experience is too far beyond the reach of a child's present ideas then the child not only fails to make sense of it but also misses a chance of advancing his or her ways of thinking. Second, arguments in favour of matching come from considering what happens in its absence. When there is frequent mismatching, children don't learn what is intended but they *do* learn that school is either boring or bewildering, a place where they can never seem to do what is expected of them. This sets up a vicious circle where failure is expected and children may develop negative attitudes. The reverse can happen when activities *are* matched to children's ideas and skills. Then the children can make sense of their experiences and gain pleasure from extending their skills and understanding. Positive attitudes to both self and school are then more likely to be formed, supporting further learning.

Common objectives and individual routes in learning

Misgivings are often expressed about the practicality of 'starting from where the child is', particularly when it is agreed that there are common objectives for all children. Does it mean that each child has to be treated individually? This seems impossible. How can we reconcile the need to move towards the objectives of learning (sometimes expressed in a mandatory curriculum) with the idea of taking children's ideas as a starting-point?

Objectives which are expressed as what is to be achieved at the end of a year or phase of schooling present no real conflict. They do not suggest what has to be reached in each lesson and so can be regarded as 'staging posts' on a journey. They are fairly widely spaced locations (represented by asterisks in the diagram below) and do not determine the path from one to another. They indicate the *direction* in which to travel but *not the route*.

1. United Kingdom, Department of Education and Science, Central Advisory Council for Education (England), *Children and their Primary Schools: A Report of the Central Advisory Council for Education (England)*, Vol. 1: *The Report*, p. 196, para. 533, London, HMSO, 1967.

A child's route from one point to the next will be far from linear; indeed, it may not always appear to be in the direction of intended progress:

Each child's route can be different but still lead in the direction of progression towards later objectives in development of concepts and skills.

When new children are received by a teacher, or a new topic started, the children may be at a range of different positions, A, B, C, etc. From each of these starting-points the teacher can begin from where the child is and help the child make his or her way in the direction of progress:

The teacher uses assessment as part of teaching to find where children are to begin with and to monitor the route they are taking.

This model describes how children make their own way in the general direction of progress. Because each child does this in an individual way (because each is an individual with unique prior experience and ways of thinking) does *not* mean that each child has to have an individually tailored set of activities. Children will make different sense of the same activities and their ideas and skills should be constantly monitored. The teacher who has information about the varying points of progress of the children will adjust the help given to and the demands made on individual children accordingly.

Assessing children's ideas
and concepts as part of teaching

The sources of information about children's performance are their *actions* (what they do or say) or the *products of their work* (what they write, draw, make or set up). Both sources give relevant information about children's ideas but the products give a more permanent form of information, which can be considered some time after their creation, whereas actions have to be assessed on the spot.

Products are more appropriate for the assessment of children's concepts than for process skills and attitudes. However, both products and actions can and should wherever possible be used in assessment of all aspects of development, since it is not difficult to realize that either source alone is insufficient. For example, it is not always possible to be sure from what children do whether their action had the purpose we might ascribe to it, but this could perhaps be checked from a written account. Similarly, what a child may write or draw can be open to various interpretations and it is often not possible to be sure what is meant without talking to the child about the product.

The key to gaining useful information about children's ideas from the products of their work is to set the tasks with this in mind. The task should give an open-ended invitation to express what the child thinks is happening, for example these drawings produced by a child aged 8 and one aged 10 when the class were studying some incubating hen's eggs. The teacher asked the children to draw what the children thought the inside of the egg would look like if they could see inside. There is a great deal about these children's different ideas about growth and development which can be inferred from these drawings. Both, however, realize that the young inside is a chicken and so have the idea of a life-cycle.

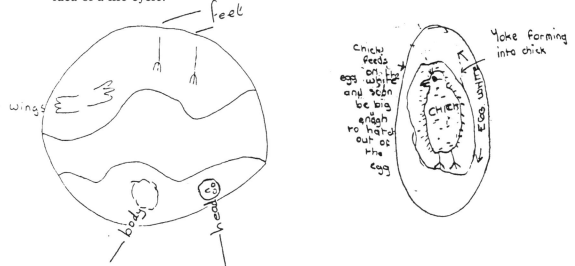

Another eight-year-old wrote her ideas as follows:

(If I could see through an egg shell it would look like a very little yellow chick.)

115

Asking children to make predictions about what they think will happen in an investigation when they are setting it up is a useful way of revealing their ideas. In the next examples, children were studying the evaporation of water. This ten-year-old hung up some 'washing' to dry on a clothes-line and predicted:

Washing.

I think that the water will run to the floor untill it drop's on the dry's

(I think that the water will run to the bottom and will drop on the floor until it dries.)

Children can also be challenged to *use* their ideas to say how a particular change can be brought about. When asked if they thought you could make water evaporate more quickly, one reply was: 'I think you can if you boil it to steam, it will go faster.'

Other children replied that you could not make it go any faster, indicating that they had little grasp of the cause of evaporation but just thought it happened 'naturally'. Similarly revealing are answers to how you could slow down the evaporation: 'By putting a piece of glass covering it and it will last longer because it can't get out.'

This technique can readily be applied to almost any event children are studying as the following examples show. *Ideas about friction*, when studying how much force it takes to pull one surface over another: 'What could you do to make it easier/more difficult to pull it across?' *Ideas about the pitch of sound* when blowing across bottles filled to different levels with water: 'How could you make a lower/higher sound?' *Ideas about what makes things float*: 'How can you make a floating object sink, or a sinking object float?' *Ideas about current* in a simple circuit: 'How could you make the bulb light more/less brightly?'

Thus, in summary, there is a range of questions which the teacher can ask which lead to children either expressing their ideas explicitly or implying ideas in the predictions or suggestions they make. The general forms of these questions are as follows. What do you think is happening when . . . ? How do you think . . . works? How do you think . . . happens? What do you think will happen if . . . ? Could we make . . . happen more quickly/slowly, more/less easily? How do you think we could make . . . happen? In all cases the questions are part of normal activities and not posed as 'tests'. Children learn a great deal from these challenges and even from the necessity of expressing their ideas either in words or drawings.

USING CONCEPT MAPS

Another technique for gaining access to children's ideas is through asking them to draw concept maps.

A concept map is a schematic relationship between concepts. Take, for example, the two words 'flower' and 'petals'. These two words can be related to each other by the use of a linking word or phrase:

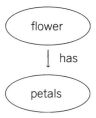

The arrow indicates the direction of the relationship – flower has petals, not petals has flower.

When several propositions indicated in this way are linked together the result is a *concept map*.

Maps drawn by children can be analysed to give information about the ideas the children have about relationships between things. The following example was drawn by a six-year-old child using the words from the list on the left (which had all become familiar from studying the growth of different seeds).

seeds
root
leaf
stem
shoot
flower
potato
water
soil
sun
bean
mung
cress
air
petals

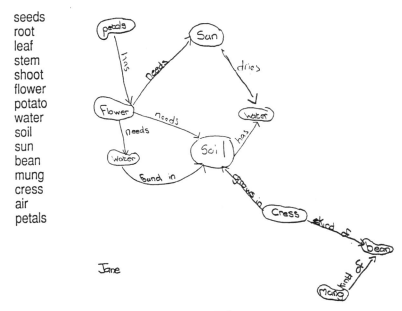

117

Any relationships can, of course be the basis for concept maps. Here is a girl's map about shapes:

shape
circle
sphere
square
cube
rectangle
cuboid
edge
triangle
prism
side
pyramid
pentagon
solid
plane
cylinder
face
corner
slide
roll
ramp
round
flat

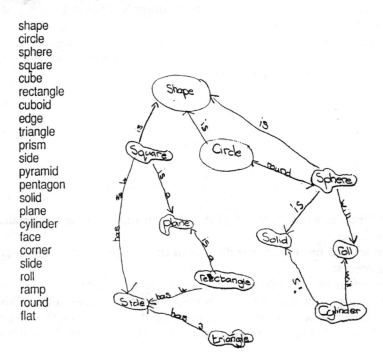

It is a good idea to try drawing a concept map yourself if you have never done so. Try making a map of the following words: hot, cold, temperature, thermometer, air, candle, oven, burn, metal, plastic, insulation.

If you compare your map with that of others you will find that no two are the same. This emphasizes the point that there are no 'correct' concept maps but each says something about how the person thinks about the relationships. You are probably aware that drawing the map makes you think hard and this is the same for children. They enjoy drawing concept maps and the result provides the opportunity for the informal assessment of their understanding in a particular topic.

One use of concept maps is to ask children to draw one of the words relating to a topic which is about to be started. Looking at the connections they make can give the teacher information about what they already know and assists in planning activities. Concept maps can also be used at the end of a topic to show what ideas the children have after relevant activities. Of course, they can be used both before and after, indicating changes in the children's ideas.

Assessing process skills and attitudes as part of teaching

Children's ability to use process skills can sometimes be inferred from their writing or oral descriptions of their investigations. However, their writing rarely includes details of how they carried out the investigation and often leaves much to be clarified. This example of a child's description of investigations with a string telephone is typical of the ambiguous way primary children express themselves: 'We went into the corridor and took the string telephone with us. We held the cup tightly and we spoke into the cup and we could hear very clearly and when we bent we could not hear properly.'

It is not clear what 'we bent' means (round a corner or just letting the string go slack?) and whether or not other factors were kept the same when the 'bending' was tried.

This ambiguity is avoided by observing what happens as the investigation takes place. This need not mean watching intently everything a child does (and worrying about what all the others are doing meanwhile!) for, with planning, the significant parts of an activity can be identified and selectively observed. Moreover, if a teacher arrives at a group when a significant part of an investigation has just been carried out, it can often be 'replayed' by asking the children to show what they did. So all is not lost when unexpected occurrences prevent a teacher from observing how a particular part of an investigation was done.

To focus observation, it is helpful to have a check-list, which has to be as much in the mind as on paper. Although the items in the examples here are expressed in general terms, not specific to any particular content, they will not necessarily all be relevant to every investigation. But the opportunity can be taken, observing particular skills when they are being used.

It will not be possible in any one session to gather information about all the children. It is best to select one group as the 'target' for assessment in a particular session. These children should remain unaware of being chosen and the teacher should interact normally with all the children in the class. The 'targeting' means that the teacher will be observing this group with the items of the check-list in mind, trying to record what is observed for the children in the group as soon as possible after the event. The record may be a simple indication of 'yes' or 'no' for each item together with a note about the particular activity being undertaken.

A SIMPLE CHECK-LIST FOR YOUNGER CHILDREN

This list focuses on the skills of observing, communicating and simple interpretation, and includes some items relating to attitudes.

1. Was at least one relevant observation made (indicated by something said or put on paper)?
2. Was something drawn or described clearly enough for it to be identified by someone else?
3. Were differences between things or from one time to another noticed?
4. Was one thing compared with another?
5. Were questions asked about what they observed?
6. Were ideas suggested, perhaps in answer to their own questions?
7. Was some interpretation made of findings by associating one factor with another?
8. Were perseverance and patience shown?
9. Were ideas shared with others?
10. Were tasks shared co-operatively?

A CHECK-LIST FOR OBSERVING OLDER CHILDREN

1. Were relevant aspects of the phenomenon observed in the initial stages?
2. Was the problem understood?
3. Was the investigation set up so that one variable was changed at a time?
4. Was at least one variable controlled (for fairness)?
5. Was the variable to be measured or compared identified?
6. Were measurements made either in setting up the investigation or later?
7. Were measuring instruments used to the accuracy of the nearest division?
8. Was at least one relevant observation made?
9. Was an adequate set of observations/measurements made?
10. Were any simple instruments used to aid observation?
11. Were results recorded appropriately at the time?
12. Were patterns or regularities in the results noticed?
13. Were actions carried out in a useful sequence?
14. Were any results checked/repeated?
15. Were generalized and justified conclusions drawn?
16. Were hypotheses proposed to explain findings?
17. Were further investigable questions raised?
18. Were sources of error identified?
19. Was perseverance shown?
20. Were ideas shared with others?
21. Were others' ideas acknowledged?
22. Were tasks shared co-operatively?

Since only a few children can be assessed in this way in any session, the teacher should choose other children as 'targets' in later sessions. It does not matter, for the purposes that we are concerned with in this chapter, that the assessment is made when children are working on different tasks and investigations. Over time, the teacher would observe all the children in several different activities and so would be able to judge the extent to which the skills were being used generally or only for certain activities. In the latter case, this finding would be important information about the children concerned and the teacher would then be able to find out what it was about certain activities that encouraged the children to use skills which they did not use in other situations. This is using the information diagnostically, as intended.

Planning for assessment

Several times we have made reference to the need to plan assessment as part of activities. This is essential if it is to have the diagnostic, formative function described here. It cannot be added as an afterthought.

When activities are planned and put into operation there are usually several stages:

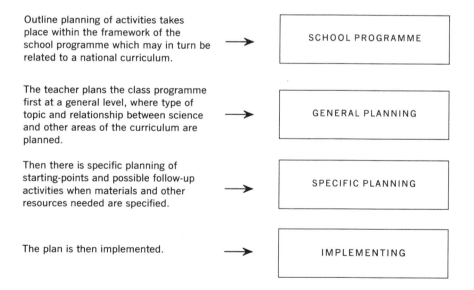

Outline planning of activities takes place within the framework of the school programme which may in turn be related to a national curriculum. → SCHOOL PROGRAMME

The teacher plans the class programme first at a general level, where type of topic and relationship between science and other areas of the curriculum are planned. → GENERAL PLANNING

Then there is specific planning of starting-points and possible follow-up activities when materials and other resources needed are specified. → SPECIFIC PLANNING

The plan is then implemented. → IMPLEMENTING

Including assessment as part of teaching is an important addition to this series of planning steps. It requires planning for gathering information about the children's ideas, skills and attitudes as part of the specific planning and the gathering of information part of the implementation. It also adds a further step of reflection (aided by record-keeping), leading to feedback into earlier steps.

The process becomes cyclic as a result of the feedback and each time assessment is used to give information about any change in ideas it is also giving information which is an input into later activities.

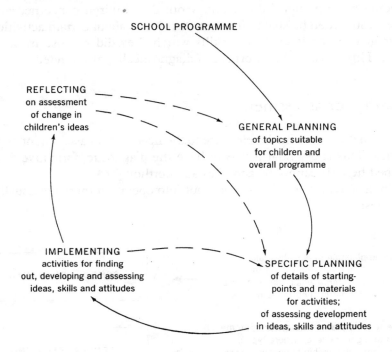

SCHOOL PROGRAMME

REFLECTING
on assessment
of change in
children's ideas

GENERAL PLANNING
of topics suitable
for children and
overall programme

IMPLEMENTING
activities for finding
out, developing and assessing
ideas, skills and attitudes

SPECIFIC PLANNING
of details of starting-
points and materials
for activities;
of assessing development
in ideas, skills and attitudes

Chapter 11

Formal assessment of scientific concepts and skills

Introduction

In this chapter we are considering the kind of assessment which was described as 'summative' on page 112. In contrast with the assessment considered in the last chapter, it is formal and takes place at intervals, not all the time.

Such assessment may be used to determine pupils' progress from class to class, for selection purposes or for reporting on achievements. Sometimes it is based on a test set within the school, sometimes on an externally set examination.

In all these cases the result is seen to be important for the children and often for the reputation of the school. This high profile ensures that the nature and content of the test has a weighty influence on the curriculum.

In practice this means that what is assessed is what is taught. However valuable other objectives may be seen to be in theory, if children are assessed mainly on the facts they can recall, then in practice in the main they will be taught facts.

The burden on developing tests which assess the full range of objectives is therefore clear. If process-based activities are to flourish and if children are to develop *understanding* and not just factual recall, then processes and understanding must be assessed.

As we have seen in the last chapter, this assessment is best carried out through a combination of observing practical work and analysing the products of children's work. However, it is not realistic to suppose that practical work can be included in formal assessment, where many children have to be tested at the same time under comparable conditions. In practice it is recognized that the assessment for formal purposes will be in the form of written tests for some time to come.

Much can be done, however, to produce test questions which assess process skills and understanding. The use of these by teachers and test developers will encourage active learning rather than perpetuating rote learning.

Questions which test understanding of scientific concepts

The factor which makes the essential difference between assessing *under-standing* and assessing *recall* is that in the former ideas have to be *used* not merely stated.

Contrast the following two questions, both related to ideas about dissolving:

Which of these dissolves in water?

sand	O
salt	O
cement	O
chalk	O

David and John put equal amounts of dry sand, soil, grit and salt in four funnels.

They wanted to find out how much water each one would soak up. So they poured 100 ml of water into each one.

This worked all right until they came to the salt. When they poured the water in almost all the salt disappeared.

Soil   Sand   Grit   Salt

Why do you think the salt disappeared but the other solids did not?

I think this might be because . . . .

. . . .
. . . .

The question on the left can be answered by recalling the fact that salt dissolves, but the meaning of 'dissolve' does not have to be understood. To answer the question on the right, it is still necessary to know that salt dissolves but, in addition, this fact has to be applied in a way which involves understanding of the meaning of dissolve. Because the word 'dissolve' is not used in the question the child has to connect it to the event described.

Look at the following examples and decide which assess recall only and which assess understanding through application.

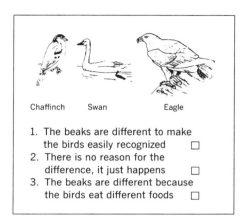

Chaffinch   Swan   Eagle

1. The beaks are different to make the birds easily recognized ☐
2. There is no reason for the difference, it just happens ☐
3. The beaks are different because the birds eat different foods ☐

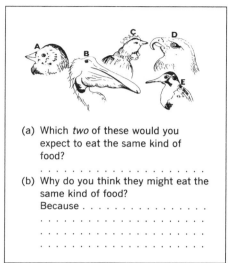

(a) Which *two* of these would you expect to eat the same kind of food?

. . . .

(b) Why do you think they might eat the same kind of food?
Because . . . .
. . . .
. . . .
. . . .

How fast do snails go?
    To find this out John and Pamela put four snails down next to each other and marked their trails.
    They put a cross (×) where each snail had reached after 30 seconds.

70 mm

50 mm

40 mm

60 mm

A B C D

(a) Which snail went fastest?

. . . .

(b) If snail C went on at the same speed for another 15 seconds how far would it go beyond ×?

. . . .

The SPEED of a moving object means:
how far it goes	○
how much force it has	○
how long it goes on moving	○
how far it goes in a certain time	○
none of these	○

To create questions that test understanding it is useful to think in terms of some general types of problems that can be set and then to translate these into questions relating to the concepts which are to be tested.

Some useful general types of question can be described in terms of the tasks they set for the children: to put given events (presented out of order) into a sequence using a scientific concept; to describe a relationship between given things in terms of a scientific concept; to give (or select) an explanation of the event which is described using a scientific concept; to make (or select) a prediction about a given situation using a scientific concept; and to make (or select) a prediction and give a reason for it.

Study the examples which follow and try to identify each in terms of these general types.

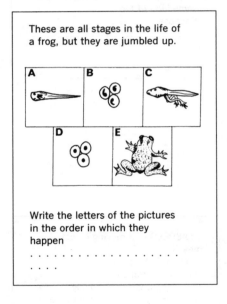

These are all stages in the life of a frog, but they are jumbled up.

A   B   C

D   E

Write the letters of the pictures in the order in which they happen

. . . .
. . . .

A food chain shows how different living things depend on each other for food. The sign B ← A means that B eats A.

Below are listed five food chains but one is not possible.

Tick in the box next to the food chain which is not possible.

☐ STOAT ← RABBIT ← GRASS

☐ OWL ← THRUSH ← CATERPILLAR ← MUSHROOM

☐ FROG ← LADYBIRD ← GREENFLY

☐ BLACKBIRD ← BUTTERFLY ← PANSY ← MOSQUITO

☐ MAN ← PIKE ← PERCH ← MINNOW ← WATER FLEA

(a) The dotted line shows where the surface of the water is in this watering can.

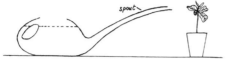

Draw a line to show where the surface is in the spout.

(b) The watering can is tipped so that the water just begins to drip through the spout.

Draw a line to show where the surface of the water is now.

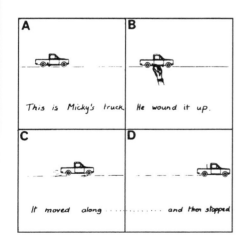

A	B
This is Micky's truck	He wound it up.
C	D
It moved along	and then stopped

(a) When did Micky's truck have the most energy?
Tick in the box next to the one you choose.
☐ A Before it was wound up
☐ B After it had been wound up
☐ C When it was moving along
☐ D When it had stopped
☐ Same all the time

(b) Give the reason for choosing the one you did.
Because . . . .
. . . .
. . . .
. . . .
. . . .

In some of these drawings the wires are connected so that the bulb will light up when the switch is pressed. Put a tick under all the drawings where you think the bulb will light up.

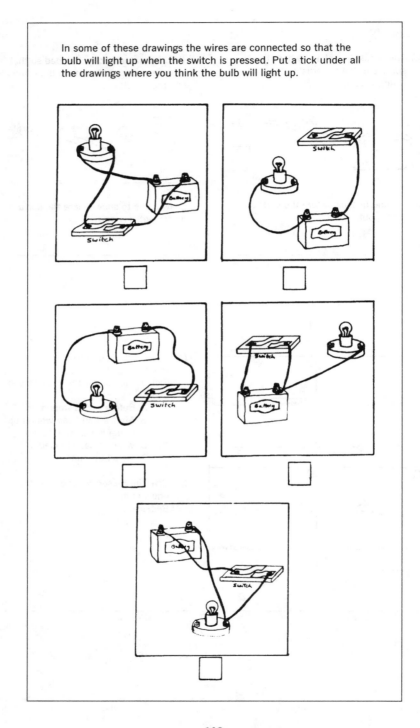

Now try creating one question of each type which would test the following ideas. Choose the type which seems best suited to the idea. You may want to create more than one question for each idea.

- Air fills the space around us.
- The moon circles the Earth, reflecting light from the sun.
- When an object is not moving, the forces acting on it are equal and opposite.
- Friction is a force which commonly opposed motion.
- Sounds are produced by vibrating objects and can travel through materials.

Assessing science process skills

Some effective questions can be created for assessing some process skills on paper. For the reasons given in the introduction, it is important for process skills to be represented in tests if they are objectives of the curriculum. However, it must be acknowledged that not all process skills can be assessed in written questions and some can be only partially covered. In particular it is not possible to include *designing* and *making* and *manipulating materials and equipment* since these must involve practical work. Nor is it valid to attempt to assess attitudes on paper. These limitations must be borne in mind when considering the following.

The key factor in assessing process skills is to create a situation in which the pupil has to *use* (not describe or recognize) the process skill involved.

Study the following series of questions about shadows.

Some children made a 'sundial' using a stick pushed through a large sheet of paper, like this:

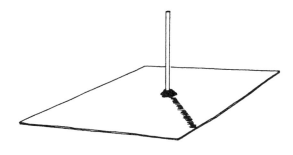

They set it up outside on a
sunny day and marked the shadows
on the paper at different times of the day.

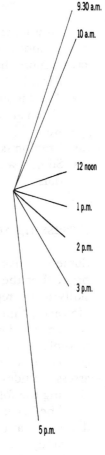

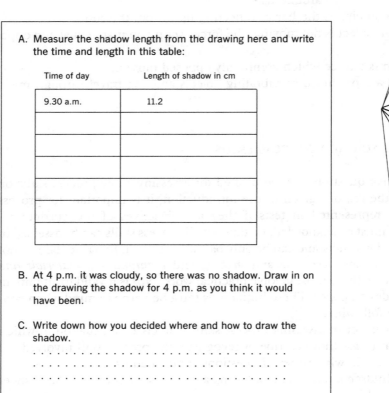

A. Measure the shadow length from the drawing here and write the time and length in this table:

Time of day	Length of shadow in cm
9.30 a.m.	11.2

B. At 4 p.m. it was cloudy, so there was no shadow. Draw in on the drawing the shadow for 4 p.m. as you think it would have been.

C. Write down how you decided where and how to draw the shadow.

. . . .
. . . .
. . . .

This series of questions assesses different process skills but makes use of the same context. Question A requires children to *measure* the lines on the drawing on their page. It also involves them in using a table for *communicating* their results. Question B asks the children to make a *prediction* and question C requires them to identify the *patterns and relationships* which can be seen in the lengths of line in the drawing. Note that these things can all be done *without* knowing about shadows and indeed even having done such an activity before would not be of much help in answering these questions.

Some of the guidelines for creating process-based questions are exemplified here: describe a situation which is familiar to the children but in which the details are unique; give a task which can only be attempted by using a process skill and avoid problems where the answer could be provided by recall.

As in the case of assessing understanding of concepts it is useful to think of general types of question which can be used for each process skill. The descriptions of these types can be readily derived from the process skill *indicators* (see pages 51–4) since these were expressed in terms of what children would be doing when using the process skills. The selection has to be made keeping in mind what can be done in the context of a written task.

General types of question for each skill are given on the following pages, followed by some examples.

Try to match the examples to the types of question and then create more questions for each process skill.

OBSERVING

Types of task:
- to use the senses to gather information;
- to find similarities and differences between objects;
- to match objects to a given description.

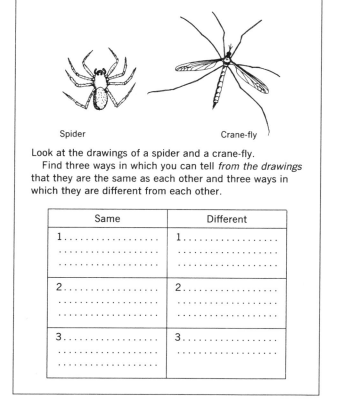

Spider   Crane-fly

Look at the drawings of a spider and a crane-fly.
Find three ways in which you can tell *from the drawings* that they are the same as each other and three ways in which they are different from each other.

Same	Different
1...................	1................... ....
2...................	2................... ....
3...................	3................... ....

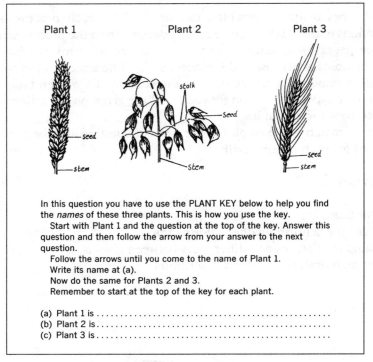

In this question you have to use the PLANT KEY below to help you find the *names* of these three plants. This is how you use the key.

Start with Plant 1 and the question at the top of the key. Answer this question and then follow the arrow from your answer to the next question.

Follow the arrows until you come to the name of Plant 1.

Write its name at (a).

Now do the same for Plants 2 and 3.

Remember to start at the top of the key for each plant.

(a) Plant 1 is . . . .
(b) Plant 2 is . . . .
(c) Plant 3 is . . . .

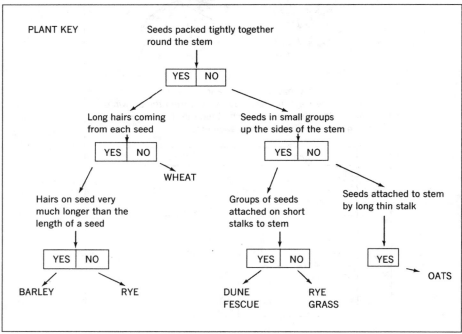

RAISING QUESTIONS

This is difficult to assess on paper and there is really only one type of task:
- to suggest questions about a given situation which can be answered by investigation.

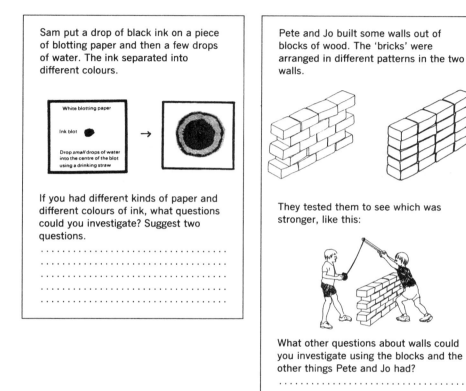

Sam put a drop of black ink on a piece of blotting paper and then a few drops of water. The ink separated into different colours.

White blotting paper

Ink blot

Drop *small* drops of water into the centre of the blot using a drinking straw

→

If you had different kinds of paper and different colours of ink, what questions could you investigate? Suggest two questions.

. . . .
. . . .
. . . .
. . . .
. . . .

Pete and Jo built some walls out of blocks of wood. The 'bricks' were arranged in different patterns in the two walls.

They tested them to see which was stronger, like this:

What other questions about walls could you investigate using the blocks and the other things Pete and Jo had?

. . . .
. . . .
. . . .
. . . .

FINDING PATTERNS AND RELATIONSHIPS

Types of task:
- to describe a pattern of relationship in given data;
- to check a possible relationship against given evidence;
- to distinguish between a conclusion based on evidence and an inference that goes beyond it.

When we cut across the trunk of a tree we see growth rings.

This tree has three growth rings.

Pith

Bark

The trees below were planted at different times in the same forest. The drawings show the trees before they were cut down and, underneath, the growth rings seen after they were cut down.

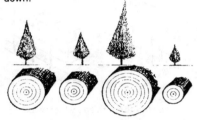

What do you notice about the heights of the trees and the rings in the trunks?

. . . .
. . . .

Julian made a model bridge out of two blocks of wood and a piece of card.

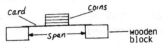

He measured the span in cm and counted the number of 2p coins the bridge could support. Here are his results:

Span in cm	Number of 2p coins
10	5
18	1
12	4
16	2
14	3

(a) What pattern do you notice between the span and the number of 2p coins the bridge could support?
The pattern I notice is . . . .
. . . .

(b) How many 2p coins do you think the bridge would support when the span is 8 cm?
I think the bridge would support . . . . . 2p coins.

Look at this picture of an apple tree in a field.

Read the statements below.
Tick the one which *you can be most sure* is true just by looking at the picture.

☐ The wind has knocked some apples off the tree
☐ There are apples on the ground and on the tree
☐ The apples on the tree are ready for picking
☐ The apples on the ground are bad
☐ The tree could not hold all its apples

134

Hypothesizing

In this case the skill involves using concepts and previous knowledge, and so there is some overlap with types of question which assess understanding. Here we give attention to types which emphasize the speculative aspect of hypothesizing.

Types of task:
- to explain a given observation in terms of a concept;
- to give more than one possible explanation of an event.

David's garden slopes down to the village playing field. Some of the trees in the playing field have branches which overhang his garden.

David noticed that the rose bushes growing underneath these branches were much taller than the rose bushes growing at the top of the garden.

David is puzzled. Can you suggest *two* reasons why the rose bushes might grow taller underneath the trees.

1. It could be because. . . . .
. . . .
. . . .
. . . .
2. It could be because . . . .
. . . .
. . . .
. . . .

Walking along this footpath Thomas noticed that there was ivy growing on the trees but only round three-quarters of the trunk. None of the trees had ivy growing on the side nearest to the path.

Think of *two* different reasons why the ivy might grow only on some sides of the trees. Write the first at (a) and the second at (b).

(a) I think it might be because . . . .
. . . .
. . . .
. . . .

(b) Or it might be because . . . .
. . . .
. . . .
. . . .

John washed four handkerchiefs and hung them up in different places to dry. He wanted to see if the places made any difference to how quickly they dried.

(a) In which of these places do you think the handkerchief would dry quickest? Tick one of these:

☐   In the corridor where it was cool and sheltered

☐   In a warm room by a closed window

☐   In a warm room by an open window

☐   In a cool room by an open window

☐   All the same

(b) What is your reason for ticking this one?

. . . .
. . . .
. . . .
. . . .
. . . .

Two blocks of ice the same size as each other were taken out of the freezer at the same time. One was left in a block and the other was crushed up.

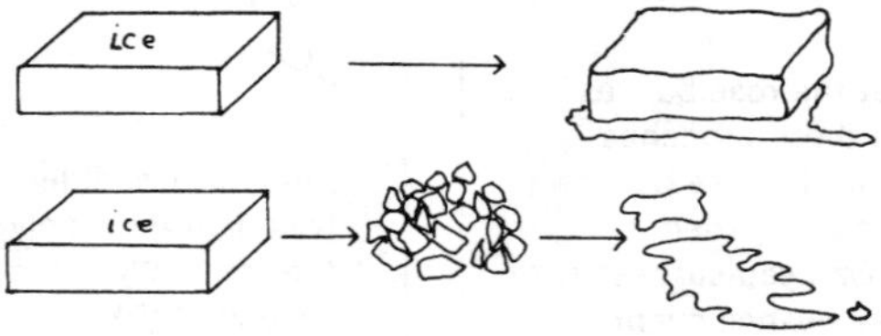

It was noticed that the crushed ice melted more quickly than the block.
Why do you think this was?
I think it was because . . . .
. . . .
. . . .
. . . .
. . . .

DEVISING AND PLANNING INVESTIGATIONS

Types of task:

• to describe how to carry out a whole investigation of a given problem;

- to identify the variables which have to be changed and those which have to be controlled in carrying out a given investigation;
- to identify what is to be measured or compared in a given investigation;
- to say how the results of a given investigation can be used to solve the original problem.

Michael made some lemonade using this recipe:

4 litres of water
2 lemons
500 g of sugar
5 g of dried yeast

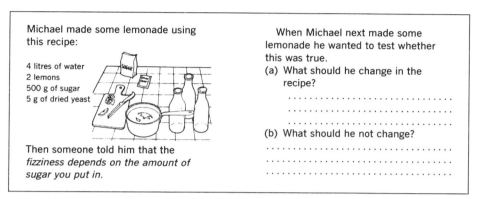

Then someone told him that the *fizziness depends on the amount of sugar you put in.*

When Michael next made some lemonade he wanted to test whether this was true.

(a) What should he change in the recipe?

. . . .
. . . .
. . . .

(b) What should he not change?

. . . .
. . . .
. . . .

Suppose you are going to make a chopping board to use for cutting bread or chopping vegetables or meat.
You have to decide which is the best kind of wood to use.
You have blocks of four different kinds of wood (A, B, C, D) and you can use any of the things in the picture below to do some tests on them. (You don't have to use all the things.)
What would you do to:

Test the blocks to find out which kind of wood is best for making a chopping board.

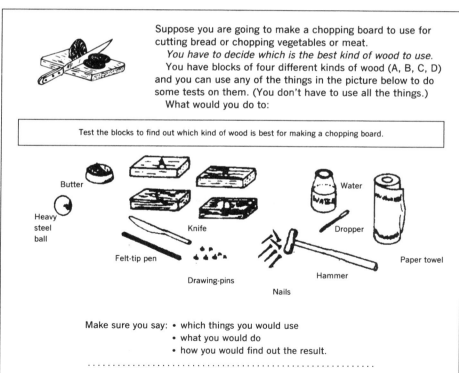

Make sure you say: • which things you would use
• what you would do
• how you would find out the result.

. . . .
. . . .
. . . .

137

PREDICTING

Types of task:
- to use evidence as a basis for saying what might happen (not by guessing) in cases where evidence has not been gathered;
- to make a prediction and explain how it was arrived at.

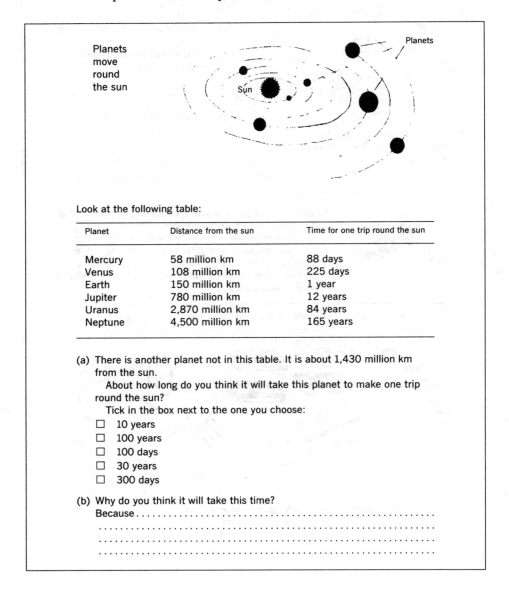

Planets move round the sun

Look at the following table:

Planet	Distance from the sun	Time for one trip round the sun
Mercury	58 million km	88 days
Venus	108 million km	225 days
Earth	150 million km	1 year
Jupiter	780 million km	12 years
Uranus	2,870 million km	84 years
Neptune	4,500 million km	165 years

(a) There is another planet not in this table. It is about 1,430 million km from the sun.
   About how long do you think it will take this planet to make one trip round the sun?
   Tick in the box next to the one you choose:
   ☐   10 years
   ☐   100 years
   ☐   100 days
   ☐   30 years
   ☐   300 days

(b) Why do you think it will take this time?
   Because. . . . .
   . . . .
   . . . .
   . . . .

In India, farmers often clear the forests to plant crops. At first they get a heavy harvest, but this gets less year by year. Then they add fertilizer, and the total weight of crops in the harvest improves, because the fertilizer puts back in the soil some of the things plants need to grow.

The bar graph below shows the yearly harvest in one area.

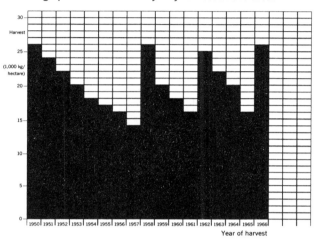

Year of harvest

Draw on the graph what you think the harvest might have been in:
(a) 1967, with no fertilizer applied
(b) 1968, with no fertilizer applied
(c) 1969, with fertilizer applied

MEASURING AND CALCULATING

Types of task:
- to measure in a given situation using appropriate units to a suitable degree of accuracy;
- to compute results from raw data.

The times of high tide at a certain place at the seaside are:

	Mon.	Tues.	Wed.	Thurs.	Fri.
Morning	6.10	7.00	7.50	8.40	
Afternoon	18.35	19.25	20.15	21.05	

What time is there between the two tides on Monday?

. . . .

What time is there between the morning tide on Wednesday and the morning tide on Thursday?

. . . .

Write in the table what the times of the two tides will be on Friday.

139

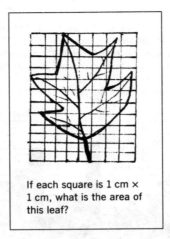

If each square is 1 cm ×
1 cm, what is the area of
this leaf?

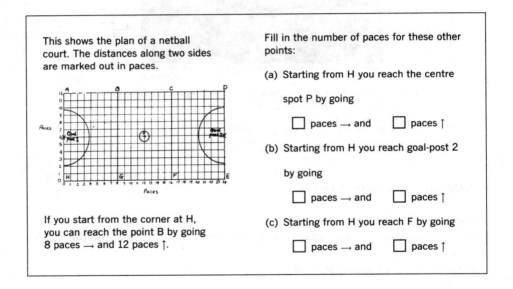

This shows the plan of a netball
court. The distances along two sides
are marked out in paces.

If you start from the corner at H,
you can reach the point B by going
8 paces → and 12 paces ↑.

Fill in the number of paces for these other
points:

(a) Starting from H you reach the centre

   spot P by going

   ☐ paces → and   ☐ paces ↑

(b) Starting from H you reach goal-post 2

   by going

   ☐ paces → and   ☐ paces ↑

(c) Starting from H you reach F by going

   ☐ paces → and   ☐ paces ↑

COMMUNICATING EFFECTIVELY

Types of task:
- to put given results into the form of charts, graphs, tables, etc.;
- to read information given in the form of charts, graphs, tables, etc.;
- to decide the best way of presenting information of a certain kind.

Richard measured his bean plant
every week so that he could see how
fast it was growing.

He started (0 weeks) when it was
just 5 cm high.

These were the heights for the
first 4 weeks:

     0 weeks: 5 cm
     1 week: 15 cm
     2 weeks: 30 cm
     3 weeks: 40 cm
     4 weeks: 45 cm

Draw a graph to show how the
height changed with time.

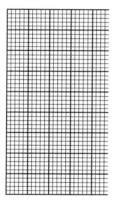

Some children measured a stream. They
called one side side A and the other side B.
They found out how wide the stream was.
They also found out how deep the water
was below the surface.

They made a graph with their results.

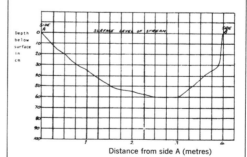

Distance from side A (metres)

Use the graph to help you answer these
questions:

(a) How wide is the stream?

(b) How deep is the stream at the deepest
point shown?

(c) How far from side A would you need to
go to get a depth of 35 cm?

To raise butterflies, you need their eggs and their food, and a cage to keep them in. (The food must be fresh.)
There is some information about different kinds of butterflies below.

Butterfly	Food plant	Egg colour	How many days for eggs to hatch	Colour of caterpillar	Colour of pupa
Small tortoise-shell	Nettle	Green, then black	5	Black with white flecks	Black, brown or green
Common blue	Bird's-foot trefoil	Pearl white	10–15	Green with brown line	Green
Swallow-tail	Fennel	Yellow, then brown	6	Black with white marks	Green then brown
Painted lady	Spear thistle	Pale green	7	Grey-black	Grey or green
Camberwell beauty	Willow, sallow	Red-brown	7	Black with red blotches	Brown

Use the table to help you answer these questions:

(a) What is the food plant of the swallow-tail butterfly?

_____

(b) Which butterfly's eggs take the longest to hatch?

_____

(c) One butterfly lays red-brown eggs. The colour of its pupa is

_____

Chapter 12

Evaluating learning opportunities in science for all pupils

Introduction

Teaching is an activity in which aspirations can never be fully achieved; there is always room for improvement. Without inducing a sense of failure, we must admit that none of us is perfect. Recognizing this, most teachers look for ways in which they can improve the help they give to children's learning.

Often there is a general 'feel' for whether things are going well, whether children are responding in the way hoped and whether they are learning. But to take action aimed at improving learning opportunities for the children requires a teacher to be more specific and to look at particular aspects of the classroom provision and interactions in a diagnostic way.

This chapter provides a means of self-evaluation which teachers can use at those points when they ask themselves 'how good a job am I doing?' It presents three check-lists relating to the children's activities, the children's way of engaging with the activities, and the teacher's actions and interactions with the children.

One of the concerns of teachers must be to ensure that as far as possible *all* children benefit from the learning activities which the classroom provides. Generally there will be some children who are clearly benefiting and this is satisfying for them and for the teacher. But are all children gaining as much as they could from the science activities? In particular, are the girls as active and questioning as the boys? Are there children who avoid certain kinds of activity, for cultural or religious reasons? What about children whose first language is not the language of the classroom? What about those with learning difficulties?

All children have the right of access to learning in science and the aim (inevitably unattainable in full) is to provide learning experiences which challenge and provide some success for all. Teachers can be helped by being aware of some of the known problem areas. Girls commonly under-achieve in science, particularly physical science, because of the male domination of the subject and the tendency to cater for boys' interests in the kinds of activities provided. Different religious groups have different interpretations of certain topics in science. Children from ethnic minorities may feel excluded when it is assumed that the conventions of the majority are the 'norm' in studying topics such as food, clothing, health and energy sources. Children with language difficulties can be helped by providing a greater range of practical experiences so that they understand directly the meaning of words and develop an appropriate vocabulary more rapidly than through the usual mixture of practical activity and discussion. Children with learning difficulties require tasks structured and paced according to their needs. They can be given access to scientific ideas and skills at levels which are satisfying to them and help in their understanding of the world around.

The process of evaluation

Evaluation is the process of gathering information and making some judgements or decisions about it. In order to make the judgements or decisions, there have to be some standards or criteria with which the information is compared. So, for example, in deciding whether a car is roadworthy, there is a check-list of information which has to be gathered about its condition and performance, and there are criteria for deciding whether it reaches the standard required. Evaluation is not as clear-cut as this example may imply. We only have to think of evaluating things such as the performance of actors, or books or pieces of music, to realize that the 'value' which the word contains plays an important part in the process.

So it is necessary to guard against thinking that an evaluation has any absolute meaning; it is always dependent on the criteria used. It is, for instance, quite possible for a lesson to be judged successful if one set of criteria is used (perhaps about how clearly the teacher presented information to the class) but less so if a different set is used (perhaps about how active the pupils were in learning). This does not mean that evaluation is not useful; it simply means that we should be clear about the basis on which any judgement or decision is made.

The process of gathering information about teaching and considering it against criteria which reflect our values and objectives should be a central concern of teachers. It is certainly essential if improvements are to be made and the whole point is, of course, to make improvements, not simply to pass judgements. Thus the criteria used will reflect this purpose and the result of the evaluation will be that some action is taken to improve future teaching.

Given this purpose and the crucial part which the criteria play in it, the best way of evaluating aspects of teaching is for teachers themselves to draw up a list of what they consider to be the 'ideal' characteristics. If there is the chance to do this, in a group with others, it is best done before reading the lists below.

Evaluating activities

Whether or not you have drawn up your own list, it is useful to consider what others have suggested as criteria for evaluating activities. The following list, which has originated in the work of teachers, will be of interest in this context, but should not be taken as having more weight than teachers' own lists. Its use is in reviewing activities which have been carried out and those which are planned.

USING THE CRITERIA

In this case the criteria are expressed as questions which are asked about each activity. They can be applied to actual events, in activities in progress, or in thinking through possible activities in planning.

Does the activity:
- give the opportunity for children to apply and develop their ideas about scientific concepts?
- give the opportunity for children to use and develop science process skills?
- encourage scientific attitudes?
- engage the interests of the children and relate to their everyday experience?
- appeal equally to boys and girls and to those of all cultural and religious backgrounds?
- provide experience of learning through interaction with things around?
- involve the use of simple and safe equipment and materials which are familiar to the children?
- involve resources which are readily available and strategies accessible to the teacher?
- involve children in working co-operatively and in combining their ideas?

TAKING ACTION

Clearly it is intended that the answers should be 'yes' to as many as possible of these questions. That will not happen for every activity and, for some, certain questions may not be relevant. However, where there are persistent negative judgements it is time to look more critically at the activities. Suggestions made in Chapter 3, for changing activities and in Chapters 5 and 6 for the activities which help in the development of concepts, skills and attitudes might well be revisited. Most help of all may come from the activities suggested in Part Two which exemplify in detail activities which meet the above criteria. These might well be taken as a pattern for activities in other topics.

Evaluating children's engagement with the activities

The concern here is with the interaction of children with the activities, not with what they have learned, which we considered in Chapters 10 and 11. The distinction is not all that easy to make, for the two are closely connected. What we are looking for here, however, is whether the children are engaging in the experiences and doing the things which give them an opportunity to develop their ideas, skills and attitudes. Again, this list is an example for teachers to compare with what they might produce for themselves.

USING THE CRITERIA

For this purpose, the questions are asked of activities which have already taken place, over a period of time (perhaps a week or two). The idea is to reflect on whether each of these has been noticed. The answer 'yes' should only be accepted if there are specific examples to substantiate it.

Did the children:
- handle materials and show by action or words that they had made observations about them?
- talk to each other in small groups about the things they were observing or investigating?
- ask questions which led to investigations?
- ask questions which indicated their interest in the way they were working or what they were finding out?
- talk freely to the teacher about what they found and what they thought about it?
- display their work and explain it to others?
- suggest ways of testing their ideas?
- discuss the meaning of words they or the teacher were using?
- consider a different view from their own and assess it on the basis of sound argument or evidence?
- carry out an investigation which they had taken part in planning?
- express justified criticism of the way in which an investigation was carried out?

- follow any instructions given to them orally or in writing without difficulty?
- make decisions for themselves about what to do?
- use equipment effectively and safely?
- measure something in setting up or finding results from an investigation?
- make a prediction based on their own ideas or findings?
- link observations in one situation to a relevant previous experience?
- show in some way that they were absorbed in their work and that it was important to them?
- use sources of information to answer factual questions?

TAKING ACTION

Whilst a 'yes' answer to these questions is desirable, there will clearly be situations and constraints which sometimes make such an answer impossible. Teachers will know, for example, whether it was the constraint of space and resources which meant that children did not have a chance to measure or use equipment. However, even in cases where there were constraints, the environment itself provides opportunities for scientific exploration, as suggested in Chapter 9, and those with ingenuity will find such opportunities within the classroom as well.

Many teachers will find that one of the greatest obstacles to providing opportunities for 'yes' answers to the questions in this list will be class size. The larger the class, the greater the noise of active learning. It just has to be accepted that a class which is busy learning science cannot be a quiet class. Learning science is not a matter of copying from the board or writing dictated notes or learning from a textbook. It is a matter of investigating, using ideas, sharing ideas, talking to and listening to others, and trying things out. There will be times which are quiet, when children are reflecting on and writing or drawing about what they have found. But the buzz of activity and discussion in groups is a must at some time.

Management skills are at a premium in large classes and science will stretch these skills. However, the teacher does not need to be in all places at once if: (a) the children know what they are doing (this doesn't mean that they are not thinking for themselves; their task can be to come up with ideas, with questions, with plans for an investigation, to report to others); (b) the activity has been structured so that the group members have well-defined roles; and (c) routines are established in relation to collecting and replacing equipment.

If group work is regularly preceded and followed by whole-class discussion, with reports from groups (as suggested in Chapter 2, for instance), then children will take seriously the accomplishment of their group tasks. With very large classes, more time may have to be spent in whole-class discussion, but there must be group work to provide first-hand experience to feed this discussion.

The second massive obstacle to working in a way which meets these criteria is time. Commonly there is resistance in practice to process-based active learning because of the type of syllabus which teachers have to cover. Typically such syllabuses comprise a long list of specific content which children have to know. Teachers feel that they have to ensure that children know each element of this list and this is difficult because the very weight of the syllabus means that there is no chance for understanding. Thus the purpose of the syllabus is defeated by its character.

A review of these syllabuses generally shows that there is potential for accomplishing their real intentions in a way which is not as self-defeating as the existing form. They can be reorganized into far fewer items which identify the key concepts which it is important to learn with understanding because they apply to life. By contrast, many of the multitude of separate facts which are listed have no relationship to the children's environment. Nothing is lost in this reorganization, but much is gained in freeing the teacher to spend much more time on the important, generally applicable ideas. Although this adjustment is not something which individual teachers can do for themselves, they may help national curriculum centres and professional associations to take action.

Evaluating the teacher's actions and interactions with the children

The third list applies to the teacher's thinking and behaviour. Considering the activities in the same period of time as for the second list, teachers should ask themselves whether they have:

- provided opportunity for children to explore/play/interact informally with materials?
- encouraged children to ask questions?
- asked the children open questions which invited them to talk about their ideas?
- responded to questions by suggesting what the children might do to find out rather than providing a direct answer?
- provided sources of information suitable for helping the children to find out more about a topic?
- provided structured group tasks so that the children knew what they were to do?
- asked for writing, drawings or other products in which the children

expressed their ideas about why something happened or behaved in a certain way?
- provided opportunity for children to present ideas or to describe their investigations to others?
- noticed children working well without help?
- kept silent and listened to the children talking?
- been aware of the children's ideas about the materials, objects and events being studied?
- become aware of changes in children's ideas from ones previously held?
- made interpretations of the children's written or other products in terms of their ideas and skills?
- kept records of the children's experience?
- assessed and kept records of the ideas and skills shown by the children?
- used the records of children's experiences and progress in planning further activities?
- talked to the children about the progress they are making in their learning?
- considered and guarded against bias in activities which may disadvantage children on account of their gender, ethnic origin, religion, language or physical disability?

The questions in this list are perhaps the most value-based of the three lists given here. They imply a role for the teacher in learning which is quite different from the traditional role as source of information. This role is consistent with the kind of learning which is the message of this book. We have to prepare our children for a rapidly changing world where they need not only to be able to apply present knowledge to new circumstances but to know how to extend their knowledge.

Our children, therefore, need learning with understanding, which by definition is learning which can be applied appropriately and imaginatively. Children learn with understanding when they take part in thinking things out for themselves and have ownership of their learning. A teacher cannot give children this learning by direct transmission, but the teaching role is none the less central, active and guiding. It requires teachers to reveal the ideas and skills children already have and to take these as the starting-points in active learning. The teacher has to help children to develop the process skills (as described in Chapter 5) which will enable them to explore their environment and test out ideas (their own and those of others) so they develop more sophisticated and useful concepts and skills in the ways described in Chapter 6.

Part of the teacher's role is to monitor children's progress and to take action where difficulties are being encountered and where challenges are too small. Teachers know what learning they wish to bring about, but the children are the only ones who can do the learning. They must remain in control so that the learning is truly *their* learning, and the skills and ideas which they develop are ones they will use in their daily lives.

A habit of self-evaluation, such as might develop in the regular use of criteria of the kind proposed here, will help teachers to reflect on their role in children's learning. It is particularly appropriate in the teaching of science, constituting a scientific approach to the constant seeking for better ways of teaching.

Using these criteria will also help us to remember, in a shrinking world, that science is international and its development in the past has depended upon contributions from many different cultures, and it will do so in the future. In our teaching, and particularly in the written materials we provide, we should reflect these contributions and avoid giving the impression that science is the preserve of certain types of culture.

PART TWO

Engaging children in active science

Jos Elstgeest

Chapter 13

Classroom activities and teacher education

Introduction

The next four chapters of this book comprise suggestions for activities which exemplify the approach to teaching and learning which we have attempted to describe and explain in Part One. Each chapter's activities concern a particular topic:

- children and water;
- children and their environment;
- children and reflections; and
- children and balances.

Of course these do not cover all the areas of content with which primary science is concerned (as proposed in Chapter 1, for example) but the purpose here is not to provide a comprehensive guide to classroom work but rather to exemplify in specific terms the things which children should do to help their learning. The presentation of the activities is also designed to indicate an effective way of encouraging children to engage in this doing. The four topics have been chosen because:

- they cover a good deal of the core ideas;
- they are of interest to children everywhere and can be applied in almost any conditions in any place in the world; and
- they require only simple and readily available materials.

The activities within the four topics have been used with children and with teachers in training and they illustrate:

- how ideas and information can be gained by active inquiry, by 'asking the water, or . . . the balance, or . . . the mirror, etc.';
- how process skills are used in this active inquiry; and
- how inquiry leads to more questions and more investigations, which in turn advance ideas and skills, which lead on . . . and on . . . to more learning.

The activities in Chapters 14 to 17 have a dual purpose: in the classroom and in the context of teacher education. In this brief introductory chapter we consider their use in teacher education and point out some of the issues of practical teaching that are best addressed in the context of actual classroom activities, for example, the use of worksheets, the identification of opportunities for developing certain process skills and the recognition of what anyone engaged on scientific activity is doing, are most usefully discussed in terms of specific examples.

What we are suggesting is that teachers and student teachers should work through many of the same activities as proposed for children, for reasons which go far beyond trying things out 'to see that they work'. We now consider the four most important of these reasons to be:

- helping the understanding of the nature of scientific activity;
- helping the understanding of how children's learning can be assisted;
- developing a deeper personal knowledge of science; and
- developing ability to criticize, adapt, extend and create further activities for children.

Such is the potential for learning in everyday things around us that the same activities which provide for young children to make steps in their learning also provide an opportunity for students and teachers to develop their ideas at a much more advanced level.

UNDERSTANDING OF THE NATURE OF SCIENTIFIC ACTIVITY

In Chapter 1 we described the process of learning as being much the same for adults as for children. There are differences in the components of the process, of course. The experiences of adults are much wider than those of children, the ideas they bring to bear in understanding new experiences are more abstract and generalized and they also have the ability to stand back and reflect upon the process of their learning. The important similarity lies in the way existing ideas and new experiences lead to the development of ideas and in how understanding results from working things out from one's own experience.

In order for teachers to be able to provide fruitful learning experiences in science for their pupils, they must recognize the nature of scientific activity. This is not easy to describe in theory, but it is easy to recognize in action. Many primary-school teachers will not have had experience of this in their own education and this must be made good in their preparation for teaching. Doing some science at their own level can start, however, from simple activities such as can be undertaken by young children. The activities with the balance (Chapter 17) provide a good example. The first few pages of the activities invite children just to play with their balance and, whilst it is not proposed that student teachers go through these elementary steps, they may well begin by investigating how the balance can be brought into equilibrium by putting different things on each side. The more precise observations which can be made using the peg-board balance (page 266) lead to the identification of relationships. Before long students or teachers are busy suggesting relationships, using them to say what should put the balance in equilibrium and testing them out. Whether or not they formulate the relationship in the formal way is unimportant. What is important is that they have found something out from the materials in front of them by manipulating, by doing and by thinking.

It is important for there to be experience of scientific activity in various contexts (as, for example, in Chapter 2 as well as the topics in Chapters 14 to 17), particularly for those who have had little experience of learning this way themselves. When they have been through these experiences, then they can stand back and examine them, and understand what makes these *scientific* activities. The experience of scientific activity is not enough; teachers must know that this is what they experienced.

UNDERSTANDING HOW TO HELP CHILDREN LEARN

The personal experience by teachers of activities which children will be undertaking can be the basis for discussing how children may tackle them and what they may derive from them. The advantages and disadvantages of particular activities can be considered in these terms. This is only possible if teachers and trainees have undertaken the same activities, including the thinking and reasoning, the searching for evidence and the making of conclusions on the basis of the evidence found.

Through their personal experience of the ideas and skills involved, they can discuss what children at different points in development will need in terms of support and encouragement from their teacher. Reflecting on how they felt themselves as learners will prepare them for what a teacher needs to do to translate activities from a page into lively learning opportunities for real children.

A DEEPER PERSONAL KNOWLEDGE OF SCIENCE

The simple activities with water in Chapter 14 exemplify how understanding can be developed at different levels. This is helpful because it satisfies the adult learner to go beyond the simple explanation which is appropriate for young children. More than this, though, it shows teachers that there is no end to the sophisticated and complex answers to the question 'why' in science and so the worry about not being able to give children the 'correct' explanation should be dispelled. What is 'right' for children is what they can understand in the light of their past experience and the evidence before them. As this experience grows and new evidence emerges, then more advanced ideas are needed and understood.

A simple activity with water, such as 'floating and sinking', carried out by teachers, may go beyond identifying things that float and sink to noticing that some things which sink can be made to float if they are placed on the surface with care. A needle or a paperclip can be made to lie on the water surface and careful observation reveals that these objects appear to make a depression in the surface of the water. An object floating in the normal way, however, such as a cork, appears to draw water up where it touches, rather than depressing it. Suggestions for comparing these things are given on page 169. The explanation for these observations in terms of surface tension may well satisfy children.

But why should water behave in this way? To go beyond the descriptive explanation requires understanding of the molecular nature of matter and the forces between molecules. This is a good opportunity for teachers to extend their knowledge of the way in which the macroscopic properties of materials are explained in terms of their sub-microscopic constituents and it may help them to explain a whole range of other phenomena. There is still another 'why', however, about why the molecules behave as they do, and we have to go into sub-atomic structure for this explanation. Recognizing that this is a stage of explanation which they are not going to understand is useful to teachers in putting them in the position of children who may be force-fed an explanation which is beyond them. Knowing where to stop in giving explanations and information is important knowledge for the teacher!

At this point it may be useful to underline certain points about what is often termed 'the necessary background knowledge' of primary-school teachers. It would be quite wrong to give the impression that this consists only of scientific knowledge. Such knowledge is necessary and desirable, to a point beyond the level of the children being taught, and it is best obtained through extension of practical activities of the kind described in the following chapters. But it is not sufficient in itself. The necessary knowledge for teachers extends to knowledge of how children learn in general and how they learn science in particular. It must include how to bring about this learning and how each activity makes its contribution to it. Intimate familiarity with the activities through carrying them out and evaluating them for themselves and then through the work of children is part of the essential and developing knowledge base of teachers.

ABILITY TO ADAPT, AMEND AND EXTEND ACTIVITIES

The introductory remarks to the activities in Chapters 14 to 17 emphasize that the activities do not form and are not intended to be used as a ready-made programme. Teachers are expected to use them to make up their work programmes since no one can do this from a distance. Whilst the general objectives of science education are the same, the details of the curriculum vary from country to country and place to place within a country. To use the suggestions here (or from other sources, for that matter) it will be necessary for teachers to accept the responsibility for adapting them to suit the circumstances of the class, the school, the locality and any national syllabus. The activities in the chapters give a helping hand but do not remove opportunities for teachers to use creative initiative.

To develop the ability to use materials in this way, it is first necessary for teachers or student teachers to carry out the activities. Then their tutor should help them to stand away from the materials and consider them critically. Some of the criteria suggested in Chapter 12 (page 145) might be introduced to consider a unit of work as a whole. It is at the level of individual activities, however, that changes have to be made and where new ideas may come up for extending activities. During activities with water drops, for example, some students realized, for the first time, how drops of water magnify. They were off to find out how much a particular drop magnifies, how this magnifying power can be increased, how the drop can be conveniently held steady so that it is a useful magnifier. Then they turned their attention to using these ideas with children, both in following similar lines of inquiry to their own and in using the product as a magnifying glass.

Trying out activities also brings insight into the effectiveness of the suggested materials. Often improvements can be suggested or substitutions made, where proposed materials are not available. A large part of the discussion in teacher education should centre around the development and application of available materials and equipment, and their appropriateness and effectiveness. If this is done from a base of trial and experience it should do much to prevent teachers' being deterred from providing practical science for their pupils on account of lack of the exact materials which are suggested.

The use of worksheets

A final general comment about the use of worksheets is in order here since the activities in Chapters 14 to 17 are presented in this form. It is suggested in some instances that certain pages can be copied for use by children. However, in general their intention is to be exemplary only and in practice altered, enriched, extended and even replaced. Teachers learn how to make these changes in workshops. So it is important to include in teacher education an opportunity for teachers to 'do' worksheets. This is fine and fun at first; it often opens up possibilities not thought of. But for an adult the worksheets provide little challenge in terms of their content. The challenge for teachers in work-

157

shops is not so much the 'doing' but in analysing what makes a good worksheet and trying to make some. Students and teachers can sharpen their skills by making worksheets for each other. When they try each others' there is a built-in evaluation.

The discussion should bring out the pros and cons of worksheets and establish criteria for a good worksheet. Some of the following points may be included in the discussion.

Pros: Worksheets are handy and help children to work independently so that the teacher is free to pay attention to other things.

Cons: How independently are the children working if they depend on a worksheet? Does the worksheet really leave room for the children's own thinking?

Problems: When children are at a loss as to what to do next after they have 'finished' their worksheet, is this not a cause for concern? Should a worksheet not end with a further suggestion, a new question, or with reference to some reading? How can we create an 'open end' so that children continue investigating and exploring?

Wording: Does the wording on the worksheet present a problem in understanding? Is it made clear when an instruction should be followed strictly or when it is just a suggestion, leaving room for children to show initiative?

Content: Are the problems proposed real ones? Will they engage the children? Are there closed questions which really need no extended investigation – such as 'Do letters change in the mirror?' or 'Can you see the things behind you in the mirror?' Such questions discourage thought and turn a worksheet into a guessing game.

After considering the negative aspects, however, it important for teachers to take a positive view. A good worksheet is not an impossibility. It poses questions in open form and not always in words. It makes clear what kinds of equipment can be used and specifies what is essential and what is optional. It gives information which may be useful but does not inhibit activity. It leads to other investigations, in various ways, perhaps by referring to another worksheet or to what children might do to extend the inquiries. It is attractive to the age-group of children for which it is intended and it provides an invitation to 'ask the . . .' to give answers to children's questions.

Chapter 14

Children and water

Introduction

Water is a common yet exciting material, freely available almost everywhere, which lends itself to an endless variety of genuine science activities. Common as it appears to be, water can be a source of wonder to children and to adults who have kept up the habit of questioning and wondering. Waterplay is one of the earliest forms of children's exploration. At normal temperatures water is pleasant to work with. Some of its properties are easily revealed and these early experiences are the start of more detailed and sophisticated ideas. 'Water makes things wet' is one of those early experiences, but that this high adhesive power is due to its molecular structure giving it a strong negative polarity is an idea which requires many more experiences and related ideas formed by reflection and thought.

All investigations of water at primary-school level can be carried out with the simplest of materials, readily available or made or improvised. Providing materials for the study of water is by itself an inviting challenge. For example, a zig-zag gutter system of split bamboo stalks or banana leaf stalks to convey water from one place to another was initiated by a practising student-teacher and carried out by a class of children in order to solve the problem: 'How can we make it easier to water our garden from the well above?' This chapter indicates many simple materials which can be used for qualitative as well as for quantitative work. Most of the things demand only the effort of collecting them. Some, however, require more careful, though simple, fashioning; for instance the making of little wooden floats of different shape, but of the same area (page 174), or the waxed cardboard shapes made to test surface tension (page 190).

Within this chapter are various activities comprising a certain sequence of experiences which are related to a particular aspect of the science of water. An

159

example of this is 'surface tension'. This phenomenon is introduced as a first experience on pages 169 and 170, where the surface tension makes a meniscus and supports a 'floating' paperclip. Little, if any, explanation of the phenomenon itself is required here. At best this may be a good time to introduce the proper term 'surface tension', but it will only stand for a still hazy concept. The concept, however, may well gain in sharpness when children have been 'heaping drops' (page 176), when they have experienced the problem of 'how full is full?' (page 177) and have measured its 'strength' with a balance (pages 189 and 190). Constant referring to and fro – to previous experiences from present ones – consolidates the idea, and helps to test whatever new notion arises from fresh experience, such as the adhesive property of water resulting in the phenomenon of capillarity and 'soaking up' (pages 185–8). By the time children have undergone and discussed various experiences of surface tension, their concept may be rich enough to make a relation between their observations, so that they can begin to seek for, and discover, a satisfactory explanation, even though it remains incomplete at this stage.

The actual sequence of activities related to surface tension is rather arbitrary, of course, but every fresh experience provides a new angle or a different point of view which is a step forward towards a better understanding of this property of water. The explanation of it in terms of the electro-magnetic forces prevailing in the lopsided structure of the water molecule will still be well beyond the grasp of children (and most teachers). But if they do recognize relationships between their observations and the outcomes of their 'what happens if . . .' experiments, they will begin to construct a pattern which gives momentary satisfaction, which is correct though inconclusive and which leaves the search open for further hypothesis and investigation. Those who later continue the quest for deeper understanding will find that the mental ground has been well prepared to foster further insight.

This chapter on the science of water brings out another important aspect of scientific activity: the recognition, use and control of variables. This ability is rather difficult to 'teach', as it requires some insight and hindsight into one's own investigative work which makes critical appraisal possible.

A first acquaintance with variability is presented on page 169. Objects of various shapes and materials float on water in a different way: some deep in the water, others high up; some fall on their side, others stay straight up. Children are asked to observe and describe these variations. So far the children are only asked to make observations, but the observations include the different properties of the objects they use, as well as the consequent difference in behaviour while floating. Something similar is called for when they compare how different shapes of wooden floats of the same area can hold different loads (page 174).

The idea of varying shape and size in turn is not included in the activity yet. Some intuitive agreement that the area should remain the same while the shape may vary is all that is suggested.

On page 176 a further step is taken when children start 'heaping drops' of various liquids onto various substances. Although 'heaping drops' basically asks for 'what happens if . . .' observations, these variables become important when results are to be compared. What can be varied are the liquid, the surface on which it is dropped and the number of drops. The results are to be found in the shape and size of the drops as they lie on the surface material. Children can see, and sometimes even measure, differences in diameter and vertical height, and they can compare the curvature of the surface of the drops. This is about as far as one can go with primary-school children: good observation and accurate recording. Nevertheless, part of the accurate recording is the mentioning of the variables: the liquid, the surface and the number of drops. Now they can establish certain facts on the basis of evidence collected. The fact that different liquids have different 'heaping' properties and the fact that different surface materials interact differently with water, spirit or whatever other liquid, are probably all that the children can conclude at this stage. But that is sufficient.

In connection with the experiments on capillarity where the 'natural flow' of water appears to be reversed, the need to *control* variables can be made obvious. This is a good opportunity to pay special attention to it, to point out once more what variables are, how this idea applies to these situations and how necessary it is to recognize and to control variables in order to get reliable results. Page 187 starts the discussion. Apart from such a discussion, it will pay off in later work to keep referring to the idea by reminding the children to look for possible variables and to take them into account in experimental work.

children

and

the science of

water

jos elstgeest

Children
and Water

Did you ever drop a stick straight down into the
water of a canal or a river?
How did it come up again?

Did you ever watch rings
going forth from a plunged·in
stone, and see them rippling
back again?
What happens where outgoing
and reflected ripples meet?

Did you ever play with a jet of water?

Did you ever fall into a ditch?

Did you ever stamp hard in a puddle?
            (and was your mother nearby?)

Did you ever make mud pies?

Did you ever watch water boiling in a
glass vessel?

Did you ever walk in a downpour?

Did you ever race sticks down the gutter?

Have you ever thought about
- how dependent we are on water?
- how much water there is all around us?
- how much water we use daily?

65%

or about how much water you are?

Then you can understand
   why this was written.

What do you need?
What can you use?

Firstly you need **water**

Secondly you need **water**

Thirdly you need **water**

And other liquids: spirit, oil, ink.

And things to put into water: salts, soap,
sugar, detergent,
colouring.

And things to put water into: tins,
jars,
lids,
jugs,
droppers,
pails,
basins,
hose,
piping,
spouts,
troughs,

And things like corks,
pins,
needles,
string,
thread,
filter paper,
blotting paper,
squared paper,
newspaper,
tissue paper,
(razor blades),
plastic foil,
aluminium foil,
plasticine,
spoons,
trowels,
pieces of wood,
wax paper,
sponges,
mop...
and a floorcloth

Did you know that you can make all kinds of useful equipment out of plastic household "bottles"? Just cut and snip away, and you get tall and flat containers, troughs and spouts, boats and buoys, sprinklers and funnels, strips and snippets, squeezers and squirters, measures and measuring jars and much more, perhaps. Be resourceful!

Infants and younger juniors

They have no use for "lessons" about water.

They would promptly stop learning.

What they need is <u>water</u>,

a little supervision and...

materials:	to do:
Funnels,	to pour,
tubes,	to fill,
straws,	to empty,
jars,	to sprinkle,
jugs,	to spatter,
vessels,	to let run,
basins,	to count,
bottles,	to drop,
tins with holes,	to drip,
with one hole,	to carry,
with no hole.	to shake,
plastic bottles,	to hold,
squeeze bottles,	to keep tight,
medicine bottles,	to squeeze,
plates,	to squirt,
saucers,	to syphon,
spouts.	to mess about,
	to play,
	to try,
	to watch.

to suck up.

can we really mess about?

and soap to blow bubbles!

And mud to make pies.

Colours to make the water beautiful.

And many more things... and odd bits and pieces...

To sink and float

to plunge and to plop!

to smudge and to smear.

Slopping and Mopping!

Oh, but it doesn't have to become a sludgy pigsty! Of course water play is fun, and spatters do splash around, but, really, it is not difficult to let even infants see the difference between a bath and a classroom!

They should **DO**.

Can you fill a bottle without spilling?

Ten egg-cups full of water fill a plastic vinegar bottle.

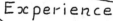

I can empty a whole bottle of water into my trouser pocket.

Experience

Have you ever tried holding this and fill it up with water.

I am sorting heaps of floating and sinking things.

Miss, when I stir everything in the water swirls around!

I am always amazed at how they always invent a syphon!

and **Wonder!**

Floating and Sinking

When children work
with water and things,
one of the first questions usually is:

"What happens if you
throw a ... (fill in what you fancy) ...
into the water?

or: What will float?
What will sink?

A very good question to start with!

However, do not leave it
at that:

Go beyond the question and WATCH:

HOW does a block of wood float?
           or a plank?

Draw it nicely.

a tin (empty)?
a tin (half full)?
a cork?
a jar?
a piece of styrofoam?
a sponge?
a ping-pong ball?

How much of it is above the surface of
                    below   the water?

Is it lying straight? or tilted? How much?

Where does a cork (or a pin) float:

a) in a full
    cup?

b) in a
   half full
   cup?

Can you make a pin,
a paperclip,
a needle,
or a razor blade float?

With a simple instrument
and a little patience and
practice, everybody can do it

Open a
paperclip

Use pliers
to make
a little
foot
and
lower
the object
gently
on to
the water

Once you get it afloat,
watch carefully once more:

How it floats.
Where it floats.

think of
the cups,
full and
half full.

try
soapy
water!

Compare a cork or piece of wood
which floats in water with the
floating paperclip;
look where floating object
and water touch!

Can you make a sinking object float?

This is a potato with matchsticks stuck into it...

How many matchsticks or toothpicks (and perhaps you can think of other buoyant things) are needed to make a potato float?

And if the potato is twice as big?

I have no matches!

And if I hollow my potato out..?

A ball of clay sinks, but I make a little boat out of it!

How can you make a stone float?

A rotten egg will float!

Whatever children suggest is worth trying out... although...

How would we do that with a stone?

Try salt water!

Can you make a floating object sink?

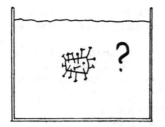

This is a small cork with pins stuck into it.
- small nails or tacks. can be used, too. -

How many pins (nails, tacks) are needed to make a cork sink?

At what pin does the cork start to sink ... and does it sink to the bottom?

At the umpteenth!

Could you make the cork float in the middle of the jar...? halfway down, I mean.

Pieces of balsawood are easy to stick pins into, and one can make measurements quite easily.

A piece of wood sinks with 15 pins stuck into it. How many pins would you need to make a piece of wood sink that is twice its size?

What size do you take twice?

Please, Miss, could you repeat this question?

How do you make a balloon sink?

Look at what my piece of chalk does when I put it in water!

Food-, fruit-, fish- and soup-tins

should never be thrown away, really,
before having been put to good (scientific)
use: - What happens if you place an empty
tin on the water surface?

 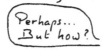

- How will it float if it is
high and narrow? ?

- How will a low and wide tin float? ?

- Can you make them all float straight up? How?

How much water,
            sand;
how many   peas.
            marbles,
            paperclips,
            pebbles,
            corks,
            rubbers.
can you load into
your floating tin
before it (just) sinks?

Is that the same for
every tin?

How come?

With 🔨 and 𝙸 make a hole
                    two holes
                        more holes in a tin...
and float it on the water.

Does it still float? For how long?
 What happens?
 What do you see in the tin?

Measure the time for one hole,
                    two.
                    four,
                    eight holes.

What happens if you put marbles
or pebbles into your tin (with one,
                            two.
                            four,
                            eight holes?

1) Measure times

2) Tabulate or graph
   a number of holes vs. time.
   b number of marbles vs. time.

Time for what?

173

Sardine-tins   bottletops   shoe-polish tins (+lids)
                jam-jar lids

are too good to be
thrown away:

they are first-class
scientific equipment
for a variety of experiments.

They can be used as "cargo boats"

- How many marbles,
             pebbles,
             sand,
             clay,
             things
can the boat carry
without toppling,
          keeling over,
          capsizing,
          or sinking ?

What else can you load?
How can you load your boat in equilibrium?

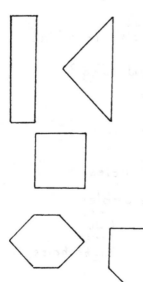

It would be nice to make
little wooden "boats",
cut out in different
shapes, but of equal
area.

o Would the shape
  of the "boat" make
  any difference to
  its "loading capacity"?

—Can you pile as many
  marbles on a square
  as on a triangle?—

o And dry sand?

o And when these
  loaded boats move?

o In how many ways
  can you make your
  boats move without
  touching them?

DROPS

How do you make drops?

Or should one ask:
How does a drop
form itself?

What exactly do drops look like?
What _is_ a drop's shape?

Observe very closely:
- a hanging drop,
- a falling drop,
- a lying drop,
- a running drop,
- a fallen drop.

If you draw
it with care,
then you know
how well you
observed!

How big is a drop?
Are all drops equal in size?

How do
you
measure
a drop?

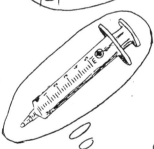

Drop
drops
into a
measuring
cup.
How many drops
make 1 or 2 ml?
So, count and divide.

Would
nobody
think of
this?

I wonder!

Once you know how to "measure" drops,
you can compare: which liquid makes
larger or smaller drops: - water?
                              - milk?
                            - spirit?
                          - sea water?
                            - oil?
                              - vinegar?
                                - soapy
                                    water?

Heaping drops

You can heap drops...
  but what happens if you do?

Try heaping one drop onto the other:

- using water
      spirit
      soapy water
      oil
      milk
      sea water
      vinegar

  on to plastic
      glass
      wood
      your arm
      metal
      foil (aluminium)
      rubber
      paper
      waxed paper
      mackintosh cloth

Look,
Compare,
and draw accurately
what you get:

a) water   ?

  on plastic ?

b) soapy water   ?

  on glass ?

c) water on waxed paper.

    1 drop 2 dr. 5 dr. 10 dr.

d) different liquids on
    waxed paper: 1: water;
    2: spirit; 3: soapsud; 4: oil.

    1   2   3   4

e) idem..   ?

  on aluminium foil.

f) whatever it is...   ?
  on whatever it is...   ?

Have you ever
tried dropping
drops on dry
sand?

Drops soak into
blottingpaper and
make rings
    - newsprint or
    coffee·filter
    can be used,
    too.

Would this be a
reliable way to
measure drops?
And to compare
their size?

What is the
difference
between drop
and drip?

176

How full is full?

Collect some small vessels:

like bottlecaps:

screw-tops:

small cups;

lids of jars...etc.

or even penholder caps:

Then try and see how many drops
of water,
of soapy water,
of spirit,
of vinegar,
of oil you can add to a "full" vessel
before it overflows.

How high can you "heap" the liquid above the rim?

You can make use of
- eye-droppers,
- injection syringes.

They are good for measuring, I told you!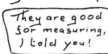

- or, if you are clever enough,
ordinary drinking straws

Which drop makes the bucket overflow?

The last one, I guess.

What happens if...
you "heap" ordinary water above the rim, but not quite as high as you dare, and then add a tiny drop of ... soapy water ?

or any other liquid.

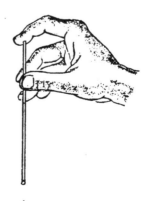

0

177

Racing Drops

Racing What?

Let drops drip and run...

- along little slopes of different angles,
- and made of (sheets of) different materials, such as plastic,
  wood,
  formica,
  glass,
  slate,
  metal,

and watch well !

Observe: how the drops run.
- Do they run straight?
- Do they run fast ?
- What does their speed depend on?

And if you change the angle of the slopes ?

Or if you use different liquids ? Oil? Spirit?

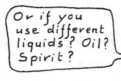

And now for the races !

Take sizeable tins, pots, buckets, bottles, or vats and let drops race each other down the curved sides.

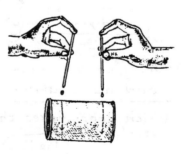

Which drop of which liquid becomes champion ?

- Can you find a way to make a drop win?

- Could you use straight-sided vessels ?

- Could you use sloping sheets ?

- How could you make drops run straight?

- Have you tried drops of ink ?

178

What more can you do with drops?

You can make a pretty good handlens:

Place a nice, clear drop on a piece of transparent plastic, (overhead projector sheet)

Try it out as a lens:
- At what distance above the object should you hold it to get it into sharp focus?

- How much (or little) can you see of your object through the water lens?

- Can you make your drop-lens any bigger? better? rounder? clearer?

- Would another liquid (e.g. oil) make a better lens?

Whatever you find: a waterdrop lens comes in handy when you have no handlens on you.

A dripping tap is a <u>clock</u>.

How can you adjust such a clock?
= How can you measure time...
... with a dripping tap?

Out of tins you can make water clocks:

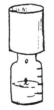

A tin with a hole? But... wouldn't you get a stream of water? And if you cover the hole with filterpaper?

You could let the water syphon through a cotton thread over the rim into a measuring jar (home-made?)

How do you wind these clocks?
How do you keep them running?

Spatters

are splashed drops.

Use coloured water

Beetroot juice is cheap.

Inks and dyes are dear.

Watercolours are expensive,

Foodcolouring "clean", but rather forbidding.

What happens with drops which are dropped from a height of 10 cm,
25 cm,
50 cm,
100 cm,
150 cm,
200 cm,

onto paper?
Wax-paper?
glass?
plastic?
stone?
linoleum?

Goodness me!
Shouldn't you rather go outside?
The mess!

or... into a pan of water?
or dry sand?

Coloured spatters you can save.
They "write" their own records...
... but you should write the "what happens if..." question next to them, otherwise you save answers without questions

You can also measure them and make a graph

Look at the question above and the spatter below!

Measure what, sir?
Graph what, sir?

If it rains,

you get many drops for nothing !

Use them!

- Watch how the rain falls :
  - straight down?
  - slanting?
  - how obliquely?
  - What would make the rain slant?

- What happens to raindrops when they drop down?
  - Look low, just above the ground, where they hit the earth
  - and where they hit the surface of a puddle
  - What, precisely, can you see happening where a drop hits the water in a puddle? (or a pan?)

Could you describe "a puddle in the rain"?
  or paint it?
  or draw it?
  or sing it, if you wish!

- What colour has the water in a puddle?
  - can you copy that colour?
  - Go and stand somewhere else: what colour has the puddle now?
  - can you copy this colour, too?
  - Look around and see if you can find something else of the same colour.

Try it

What is hard when it rains hard?

If it keeps raining...

- What does the rain,
  or the rainwater,
  <u>do</u> to the ground?

What would
cats and dogs
do to the
ground?

- Look on the path,
  · on a bare patch,
  · in the sandpit,
  · under the tree,
  · in the grass.

Where does the rainwater
leave the clearest tracks?

Did you look where the ground
slopes?

Could you make
a mini-river system
yourself on a sloping
sandy patch of ground?
Even on a dry day?

- Where does all the rainwater go?
  · How do you know?
  · Can you think of some way to "follow"
    the water?

Are all raindrops equal in size?

Stick a piece of paper outside; hold it
flat into the rain... for just one second...

- What can this bespattered paper
  tell you? ...about equal or unequal sizes?

- How many drops did you catch?

- Could this small experiment tell you
  something about (what is) "gentle" rain
  or "hard" rain?

- Measure the biggest spatter,
  the smallest,
  the one which occurs most.

What exactly happened to the raindrops
hitting the paper?
Does this also happen when they hit glass?
plastic? stone? dry sand? a mackintosh?
a handkerchief? bare skin? kinky hair?

The Mathematics of a Shower of rain.

This is heavy rain!

How do you measure rain?

With a raingauge, of course!

How "of course" is the raingauge?

What do you want to measure?

- The size of the drops?
- The amount of drops?
- The quantity of water that has fallen?
- The amount of rainfall at a given time and place?

What _can_ you measure

- With a rain gauge?
- With a good, straight-sided, tin?
- With your "spatter-paper"?

What means: "3 mm rainfall?"

The rest you have to calculate or to estimate.

Now calculate:

An estimate is like a measured guess

a) The area of the school's playground.

b) If the rain gauge measured 2 mm of rainfall, how many litres of water fell on the playground?

And if the whole shower fell on an area of 1.5 square Kilometres, and measured 2 mm, how heavy was that shower?

If n drops drop on your paper (A4) in one second, how many drops, then, drop on your playground from a shower lasting 10 minutes?

Water and Dye

Water is a fluid...
...but how does it
flow?

Movements and currents
_in_ the water are usually invisible...
until you drop a crystal of dye,
or a drop of colouring (or ink)
into the water

What does happen if
you drop a drop of
dye or ink in a glass,
or a basin, of water?

TRY and WATCH

By this simple technique
-or trick- you can draw quite
a few secrets from the water:

- How does water move?
- How does water mix with
  another liquid?
- How do currents run, or flow?
- How does the water at the top
  of the kettle heat up?
- How long does water which has
  been stirred turn round and
  round?
  - or how long does water "remember"
    in which direction it was stirred?
- How does a crystal dissolve
  in water?
- How does a dissolved - or a
  dissolving - substance (:solute)
  spread through water?

Water
and dye
help you
solve these
problems.

through moving water?
through still water?
through cold water?
hot water?
heating water?

Water running upward   ?

Take two small glass plates,

and, at one end, you stick
a match stick between them.

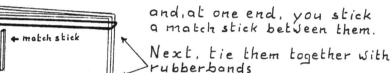

Next, tie them together with
rubberbonds

Now touch, with the underside
of this contraption, the surface
of the water in a basin ---

What happens to the water
between the glass plates?

Draw it.   Describe it.

What happens if
you stand a brick
in a plate, pan or
pot of water?

- or a rock?
- or a broomstick?
- or a piece of chalk?

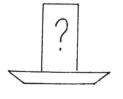

Let water climb

up a strip of paper

and you will find
many problems
to be solved by
as many experiments:

In what paper does the water
climb highest?

· In blotting paper?
· In newspaper?
· In copybook paper?
· In kitchen paper?
· In wrapping paper?
· In wallpaper?
· In toilet paper?
· In filterpaper?

· In doesn't-matter-what-paper?

If you hang
these strips
in a row, you
automatically
get a graph.

And how does
water climb
- high or low -
in strips of
· cotton cloth?
· wool?
· nylon?
· plastic?
· felt?
· canvas?
· muslin?
· linen?

I try it in
· coloured water
· sugar water
· salt water
· oil
· spirit
· lemonade
· milk

... if I am
allowed to...

And in strips
of trouserleg?
of shirtsleeve?
of coat tail?
of an old sock?

Variables

A variable is a quality that may or may not differ.

If you want to make valid comparisons, and so assure yourself of dependable solutions to your problems. you should compare only one possibly different quality at the same time.

Example 1: to solve the problem:
"Which liquid rises highest?"
you may use:

different liquids,

and put them in the same place!

but: the same paper
of the same width,
dipped to the same depth in the liquids.

Example 2: to solve "How does the width of the strip affect the rise of the water?"
you must use the same kind of paper and the same liquid, and dip the strip to the same depth in it.
Only the width of each strip may differ.

This is called "Controlling the variables" in an experiment.

) control a whole bunch of variables every day!

Keep this in mind, and you can solve many problems.

Like: How fast does a liquid rise in
(How far)   - different papers   ?
          - different textiles ?
          - different bricks   ?

And: How fast do different liquids rise in --- papers ?
                textiles ?
                bricks ?

How would you control variables here?

And there are plenty other problems:
Listen!

How come the liquid stops after a while? Does it dry up?

Would it get higher up if we wrap thin plastic foil around our strips?

You can hang your strip inside a bottle and cork it!

I can let water creep over the side of a jar through a thread of cotton.

I am going to make a strip of filter paper, and let the water move around a blot of ink

How does water move up a round piece of paper? Or through a star-shape, or a zig-zag?

I put three colours in my paper-strip

I make a paper with a hole in it! No, three holes, ... no, four!

How "strong" is water?

- You can "heap" waterdrops.
- It carries paperclips, needles, razorblades.
- Water "pulls" itself up.

Is water "strong"?

How "sticky", clinging, or tenacious is it?

And have you ever tried to separate two wet plates of glass?

Cut this shape out of paper.

and fold the tail zig-zag:

and you get a water surface tension meter.

It also "measures" possible surface tension of other liquids: at least you can compare.

Just touch the surface, and gently pull upward: how far does the zig-zag-spring extend?

Can you think of a more reliable instrument?

I would try a light springbalance

Wouldn't it be better to use something flat with it?

Yes, because there is more surface for the water to hold on to!

Or... shall we use a proper balance?

- - -

How about adding washers to a floating razor-blade?

189

The surface tension balance

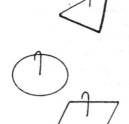

Cut regular shapes out of strong paper or card — which you can make waterproof by dipping it in hot candle wax — or out of plastic or metal sheeting.

Fix a pin through each figure's centre point, and bend it to make the shape suspendable, and keep it in balance.

Suspend one figure, on a thread, from the balance, and bring the balance to equilibrium first. Then let the shape just touch the surface of the water.
Now add units of weight (e.g. paperclips) to the other balance-arm, and count how many are needed to pull the shape free from the water('s hold).

Now you can compare and find out to what extent shape, size (=area), or even kind of liquid, affect the liquid's (the water's) "holding power".

Mind the Variables!

when you consider solving problems like:

· Is soapy water stronger, or..?

· Is one shape held more "tightly" than another?

· How can you compare the water's pull on different areas?

Which Variables should be kept constant, and which one may vary?

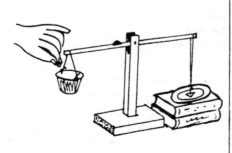

Try and make different shapes with the same area, and different areas of the same shape.

ICE, WATER, STEAM

Where does boiling water go?   Can you retrieve it?

There is a classic experiment whereby a cold plate is held in the jet of steam coming from a whistling kettle...

I find this rather dangerous for children! Even teachers burn their fingers!

A surprising investigation is:

> What happens to the water's temperature between ice and steam?

- Start with a pan of iceblocks (+ water).
- Hold a thermometer in it and from now on take a reading every minute.
- Keep a careful record of the temperatures.
- Heat the pan on a steady flame, or on a hotplate, and let the water boil for at least five minutes.
- Make a graph.
- What does this graph tell you?

temperature in °C

?

time in minutes

My children love making ice cubes in the freezing compartment of a refrigerator.

I have sent them off with the problem of making ice balls, or ice eggs, or ice rings, or, indeed, any shape.

Miss, how can you keep the airbubbles out of the ice blocks?

191

Evaporation and drying up.

Drying the laundry seems so common, but what exactly happens when the wet clothes dry?

What <u>is</u> "drying up"?
How wet is wet?
How dry is dry?

Can you measure wetness?

Out of a simple balance you can make a good wet-and-dry meter:

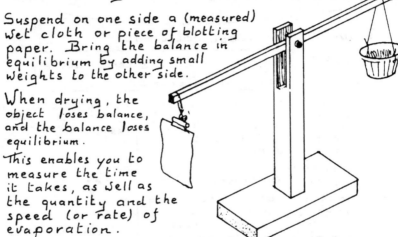

Suspend on one side a (measured) wet cloth or piece of blotting paper. Bring the balance in equilibrium by adding small weights to the other side.

When drying, the object loses balance, and the balance loses equilibrium.

This enables you to measure the time it takes, as well as the quantity and the speed (or rate) of evaporation.

(P.S. Weigh the dry object first: then you know how much water it still retains: $1 cm^3$ water is 1 gram)

Now, thinking of variables (which ones?) you can solve: 1. Does the place (position) make any difference?
   In the sun? the shade? the draught?
   On the cupboard? In the corner? Under the table?

   2. Does the shape make any difference?
   Circular? Square? Triangular? Ribbon-like?

   3. Does the area affect the rate of drying up?

N.B.: Cut same shapes, different areas;
   same areas, different shapes.

Is this the end?

There is no end, of course, because many questions and problems remain.

There is much more to be done with, and much more to be learned from, water.

Think of: - Waterpower
- making turbines;
- study erosion;
- work on pressure;
- hydraulics.

- Water cycle
- Water preservation
- Waterworks
- make a water-distribution map;
- dismantle and assemble a tap.

- Water pollution & purification
- Filtering.

- Solutions and Solvent (s)
- How many sugar lumps dissolve in <u>hot</u> water? cold
- What do you get if you evaporate sea water?

And whatever lives,
           lives not,
           lives no more
in the world's waters.

Everything is important,
          is interesting,
          is instructive,
          is relevant.

Fit in any topic which catches your children's attention, or yours.

Just get started, and see where it ends.

Chapter 15

Children and their environment

Introduction

The environment of every school is full of interesting features, full of information and full of illustrations. It is also rich in materials to work with, almost all for free. As a rule, the school environment is very close (and appropriate) to the daily experiences of the children in their own familiar world. The familiarity of the environment might be a drawback in so far as it can lead to taking things for granted. Some effort is therefore required to delve into the unknown parts of this well-known place.

This effort is required from the pupils in the first instance, for they must learn to ask questions which are not always obvious in an everyday environment. They must also learn to look for and find satisfactory answers to their questions. Fortunately, answers to appropriate questions are hidden within this environment and can be uncovered with the right kind of scientific exploration and endeavour. Whatever the children uncover, they also discover, and they delight in discovery. This kind of discovery through scientific endeavour and discipline takes away the odium of randomness, often mistakenly associated with the idea of 'discovery learning'. Endeavour can be planned.

This means that the teacher, too, must make an effort. Not only does the teacher have to make a biological or ecological survey of the school's immediate surroundings, he or she also has to recognize and measure its potential for children's activities in their learning of science. It is the teacher's task to stimulate, and often to formulate, the questions or problems with which a living environment confronts children.

This chapter presents a number of suggestions and ideas about doing science in the neighbourhood, in the surroundings and in the environment. It attempts to give an answer to the question: 'How can we help the children to use their own environment as a source of learning?'

It does not provide 'ready-made lessons' simply because it would be impossible for an outsider to make these up. Every school's environment is different from all others and therefore unique. Having explored the school environment, teachers must make their own activity plans according to the possibilities and opportunities offered by this environment.

The aim should be to help the children to approach their environment, or aspects of it, with a new scientific look, so they learn to view it as a whole, in all its complexity. Some activities suggested in this guide do just that: working on a minifield, or a transect, means observing it as a community in which we try to unravel relationships and interdependence, and other influences. We start, however, direct from the touchable, observable and very concrete materials and situations of our children's real environment.

On pages 201 to 203 are ideas, often in the form of questions, about how to study a minifield (a small patch of ground, clearly demarcated in some way) and how to relate observations to each other to find relationships. Questions are suggested which can be answered by looking carefully and which will, of course, lead to other questions. Variations in the study of minifields (page 204) are proposed as starters; teachers and children will think of many more.

What is suggested for working with minifields is of equal relevance to the other activities and exercises described in the chapter, since they are basically similar in approach and technique to the study of minifields. They lead, however, to more comprehensive results and, hopefully, to pleasant and motivating surprises. Some such surprises were expressed by a group of teachers who, during a workshop at their school, attempted the exercise named 'A Biofield in Layers' (page 205). An interesting area was chosen at the edge of a stretch of woodland where the undergrowth began to give way to open grassland. The teachers were told to study the area in detail, to sample samples where desired and to prepare an accurate map, illustrated with sketches, drawings or real samples.

The first group was assigned to the area 'underfoot'. This meant that they studied no more than the soil and what was immediately on it or in it. Their attention was drawn to the thicker layer of humus in the wooded part, of which they took a sample for display together with their presentation afterwards. They also dug up a number of roots and root systems, rhizomes and creepers, which on closer scrutiny revealed not only a surprising variety, but which also clearly indicated a visible relationship between form and function. What they had formerly dug up from schoolbooks they had now dug up for real, and their comments expressed satisfaction: 'I am going to do this with my children.'

Members of the second group, restricted to the lower five centimetres just above the ground, were surprised at finding species of plants which grew no taller than a few centimetres, yet were complete: flowering and seeding. The elbowing action of leaf rosettes came to their attention and the question

'Where does the stem of a plant begin?' led to a fascinating investigation and discussion. The group studying the layer between knee- and shoulder-height became interested in the aerodynamics of a swarm of midges dancing above the grass, something they would normally have passed by without noticing. The group mapping what was found above eye-level expressed surprise at the great variety in size, colour and even shape in the leaves growing at the ends of branches of shrubs of the same species.

These teachers, like most others, were not field biologists, but they were motivated by the unfamiliar approach to something they had walked by for ages without taking much notice. The most pleasant surprise, however, came when they presented and displayed the records of their findings: five annotated maps, filled with sketches and fresh samples, which contained so much more information than they had expected and revealed such a high degree of creativity that they made two comments: 'Can so much information be found within so small an area?' and, looking at the five very different representations of this same area: 'Have we done all this?'

Working on a transect (pages 206 to 209) leads a step beyond the closer community of living things in a minifield. A transect is more suited to the study of the vegetation across a larger area; it gives an overall view rather than great detail. A sequence of changes in vegetation across a piece of land can often be related to visible conditions like the composition of soil, exposure to wind or sunshine, tilt of the land, or disturbance by passers-by or cultivating machinery.

When studying 'vegetation', one considers the collective plant cover rather than individual plants. Vegetation is more than just the plant cover of an area. It gives the landscape (or landscape elements like an embankment, the verge along a country lane, or the swampy edge of a pool) its own colour and character, along with prevailing physical and climatic conditions as well as the influence of inhabitant fauna. The lonely ant who happens to pass by is of little importance, but the wriggle of eating caterpillars certainly is to be taken account of.

From page 210 onwards, attention turns from the field to plants as individuals. Considerable emphasis is placed on using the actual plant as a first source of information about itself. What does the plant *tell* about itself? To answer this question, which keeps returning in different guises, the student (child as well as teacher or trainee) is required to observe the plant and its features accurately and in great detail. However, observation is only a first step, for the student must now attempt to look through what has been observed in order to gain insight into such relationships as exist between form and function of various plant structures, or between the plant and outside (situational) influences. This requires thinking and reasoning, putting acquired concepts in order so that an intelligent hypothesis can be formed and formulated. It calls for comparing and finding similar structures related to similar functions. Further work may lead to simple experimentation.

The role of language (plant words) is placed in its proper position: as a vehicle of thought and a means of communicating findings. Classification of plants is presented not as a matter of fact and a completed system, but as an activity to be done, requiring skills of observation and ordering. When classifying plants, students observe similarities and differences, and by discussion they establish criteria for grouping their plants on the basis of observable characteristics. This means that they must make decisions on which features are relevant to establish 'likeness' or 'difference' in relation to inclusion in, or exclusion from, a certain group or 'class' of plants. Linnaeus might smile at the result of such activity done by a group of children, but he would be delighted by the method.

Finally, some activities on animal life are suggested with great emphasis, once more, on observation and finding relationships, particularly with the environment.

Children

do Science

in their ENVIRONMENT

Jos Elstgeest

Children orient themselves in this world. Continuously they try to accommodate themselves among the many living and non-living things, forces and powers, mishaps and successes, natural phenomena and unexpected events, illness and bad weather, joy and grief. They are surrounded by multitudes, and they want to make sense of it all by figuring out relationships, connections and explanations. They adjust themselves and their behaviour accordingly. They try to conquer their world by attempting to understand it in all its multiplicity and complexity.

The environment is the children's own: they live in it, they play in it, they belong to it, they are familiar with it, and they learn in it. This familiarity may give the false impression that they know all about it. They do not, of course, and they have to be prodded to learn more from it, and so about it.

In these worksheets you will find a number of suggestions and ideas about doing science in the neighbourhood, in the immediate surroundings, in the environment. They attempt to give an answer to the question: 'How can we help children to use their own environment as a source of learning?'

You will not find 'ready lessons', simply because it would be impossible for an outsider to make these up. Every school's environment is different from all others and therefore unique. Explore your school environment, which you share with your children, and make your own activity plans according to the possibilities and opportunities offered by this environment.

Help the children to approach their environment, or aspects of it, with a new, scientific, look, so they learn to view it as a whole, in all its complexity. Some activities suggested here do just that: working on a minifield, or a transect, means observing it as a community in which we try to unravel relationships and interdependence and other influences.

We start, however, directly with the touchable, observable and very concrete materials and situations of our children's real environment.

Working on a minifield

- Choose a piece of ground which, for some reason or another, looks interesting.

It need not be of uniform appearance.

Use sticks, slats or string to mark or peg out a square of, say, 1×1 metre.

I use a hoop, that gives me a round square metre.

Now study this minifield carefully and map it:
- What lies there?
- What sits there?
- What moves there?
- What crawls there?
- What creeps there?
- What grows there?
- What digs or dug there?
- What lives there?
- What made a home there?

This is nice group work! Let's work together on it.

If you take a convenient shape and measurement, then it is very easy to map things accurately: various kinds of plants, objects, stones, holes, seeds, fruits, seedlings, animals, droppings, peels, throw-aways, and other bits and pieces.

I lost my red pencil recently...

Try and see

if you can find <u>relationships</u>
between any of those things you find in
your minifield:

Relationships ...
... between individuals of
one kind.

... between different kinds.

... between plants and animals,
... between plants and people,
... between plants and things.

... between animals and people,
... between animals and things,

... between things and people

Could you write down what you find or think?
You may draw, or sketch, or paint to make it clear.

Better: talk about it first:

Look also for relationships
between (things within) the
minifield and (those in)
the larger world without.

Perhaps
somebody
passes through
your minifield..

- Where from?
- Where to?

Seedlings come from seeds ...
  From where came the seeds?
    Can you find parentplants around?
      Where? Many? Far away?

Leaves lying about ... were blown from where?
 Can you find trees somewhere near?
 Do they have similar leaves?

Look carefully, too, at what sits and lives
underneath, and at the bottom of
your minifield ---

And do not forget to look
 at what hangs above it.

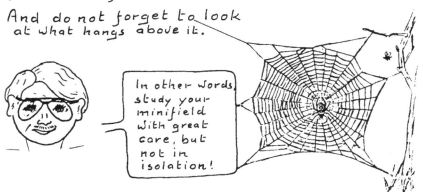

In other words,
study your
minifield
with great
care, but
not in
isolation!

If the children compare their findings
recorded on their minifield maps,
it would add meaning to their conception
of the character of a larger area.

Minifield and Maxi-use.

My little ones love choosing pretty, flowery minifields... and then picking them bare!

Mine just make their own minifields: if they find there is no flower, they go and pinch them from elsewhere!

My children studied minifields at the edge of a wheatfield. Surprise! Try it, too!

My nine-year-olds just love separating and sorting "sorts".

We made a vegetation study of 3 larger areas: a wood, a hillside-wasteland, and an embankment, by sampling and comparing minifields. Then we spread out all maps in the assembly-hall.

My class "adopted" minifields for a year. Each child returned to his or her "own" minifield every season and kept good records of what was changed and what was permanent.

A long string of minifields works like a transect and it does not have to be a straight line.

Our teacher gave each of us a minifield to weed in his garden! We could keep the weeds, he said.

204

A Biofield in Layers.

Look for an interesting spot somewhere nearby where there is plenty of growth.

A what?

Peg out a small area of some 2 x 2 metres.

Ten to fifteen children (students) can work on this.

Form small groups and divide the work: to map this area in 5 layers.

Group I maps the area underfoot.

Group II maps the area as far as the ankles reach.

Group III maps the area up to kneelevel.

Group IV maps the area at shoulder level.

Group V maps the area above eyelevel.

· Collect your information with care: whatever you find noteworthy.

· Make notes and fill in a rough sketchmap.

· You may (where this makes sense and is not sinful) collect samples.

· Take everything back to the working table (classroom) and complete the map of the assigned "layer" and embellish it with relevant samples.

It helps to subdivide the map of the area.

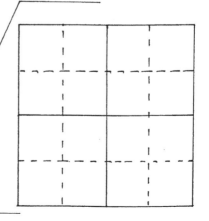

Working on a Transect

A transect "cuts across", makes a transverse section of, a piece of land: a landscape.
It is a means of making a more global study of a larger area: more detailed than an overview; less detailed than a minifield.

Choose an interesting stretch of land in an area which shows some transition:

e.g.:
- changing vegetation
- the edge of a cultivated field.
- across a ditch, a dune, a dike, a dam, a wall, an embankment: (usually to compare influences such as exposure to sunshine or shade, or steepness or swampiness or...)
- the edge of a wood

Span a string across the area or feature you wish to investigate.
Limit your observations to a maximum of 20 centimetres, or less, on both sides of the string.

For beginning children it is good to use colourful ribbon. I often stretch two ribbons or strings, about 30 to 40 centimetres apart, running parallel.

I tie knots in the string at one-metre intervals. This makes it much easier to locate features accurately and to map them correctly afterwards.

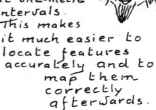

Oh, they find it too difficult to leave out something interesting which is "out of bounds".

Now for the difficult part:

A transect is meant to bring the investigating child nearer to understanding the web of inter-relationships between living and non-living things and all sorts of other influencing factors. This might begin to reveal something of the nature of transition and change.

Right, but first things first:
Children must first learn to register carefully and properly those findings which matter, which are relevant.
They must be helped to find what is relevant.
Questions and suggestions like those that follow will help.

There is one general question, to which all questions of detail are related, and that should be kept in mind throughout:

"What do the things, the changes, the differences, the occurrences along this line "tell" me about this stretch of land and what lives on it?

Shall we take plastic bags with us?

What for?

Well, to pick up rabbit-droppings!

Questions to keep looking...

- What grows/lives here?

- How does it grow?   in clumps? in bundles?
  climbing? twining?
  creeping? spreading?
  ... or firmly on its own?
  solitary?
  or many together?

- How many plants of the same kind?

- How many of a different kind?

N.B. a kind is
often called
a species.

If you cannot
count them,
don't worry:
just describe
that in terms
of "many",
"more" or "most"

- Are all plants of
the same species
of the same height? or the same colour?

- In what does it all grow?

- Where you see a change, e.g. of vegetation,
does the soil show a difference, too?
In colour? in composition? in texture?

- Which other things obstruct or influence
growth of vegetation?   · rubbish?
                          · rocks?
                          · passing people?
- Is the land facing   · water?
  · North?   · burning?
  · South?   · cutting? or moving?
  · East?
  · West?
  · the sea?
  · a mountain?

How warm (cold) is it here?

How wet,
How moist,
How humid
 is it here?

at grassroot's level?

How open?
How overgrown?

How sunny?
How shady?

Where is "here"?

How windy?

How far was this area left undisturbed? Or trodden? Or flattened? Or mown, picked, eaten?

How do the plants "move"? Upward? Sideways? Spiralwise? Do they root at every node?

Do not forget: trees are plants, too, and so are the algae growing on them; so are the mosses, liverworts, toadstools, moulds, lichen...

Do you find bulbs, tubers, rhizomes in the ground? Are any fruits or seeds attached to the plants?

Do other creatures (or things) lie about, move about, creep, dig, bore, cling, stick or hang about?

What did walk, sit, gnaw, eat, spit, defecate, moult, shed hair, or leave other things or tracks?

<u>Remember</u>:

These are guiding and "helping-to-look" questions. You cannot measure everything everywhere.

Sample data where you find them relevant, e.g. to compare one end of the transect with the other, or a lower part with a higher.

Measure temperatures: underground (to 5cm) and on the ground.

Measure relative humidity off the ground and among the vegetation.

Soil can be smeared on paper (the map!) to show its colour.
To preserve substance and texture, "trap" a little soil under scotch tape or a tiny plastic bag stuck to the map at the right place.

To map a transect use a long strip of paper. Indicate the metres (knots!) on a convenient scale, so you can keep relations of space and size with accuracy.
Map your findings (sketches, samples, notes, smears) carefully, either on a proper map (bird's-eye view) or a longitudinal section (side view).

What are
little plants
made of?

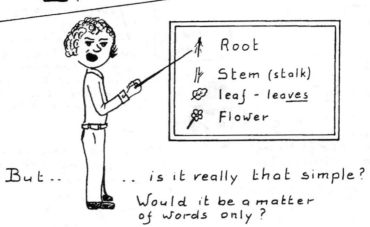

↟ Root
⇂ Stem (stalk)
❧ leaf - lea<u>ves</u>
❀ Flower

But..   .. is it really that simple?

Would it be a matter
of words only?

What exactly do you know when you can
recite this short list?

And the plants
themselves...

a little
language,
that's all.

What can they tell us?

Does not every plant tell us its own story?

But you cannot
study each and
every plant!

Of course you can
not, but you
can learn to
"listen" and
be observant
to what the
plants have
to "say".

Start by paying attention
to the structure of the
plants you meet:

How do form and function relate?

Form and Function

What does (the) form reveal
about (the) function?

When investigating plants and their parts,
keep questions like the following in mind:

- What does it look like?
  - What does it resemble (if anything)?
- How is it "put together"?
- How do its parts fit together?
  - How are they joined?
  - Space, distance, angle?
- What does the plant consist of?
  - Wood? Fibre? Edible green? Coloured parts?

Especially when considering parts of a plant:

- What could be its function?
  - What purpose does it serve?
- Is this its function?
- ...What makes you think it is?
- Could you verify this? How?
- Could it be different?
  - Are there different forms
    having the same function?
  - Are there similar forms
    having different functions?

Thinking,
Hypothesis,
Experiment.
That is good
Science.

What do we
do with such
abstract quest-
ions?

Well, find a
plant and
make them
concrete.

There are various ways of doing this.
Two examples of possible activities follow.

211

I: Ask and Compare

Go outside and collect some (3 to 5) common plants. Dig them out carefully, wash and rinse them and put them down one next to the other---

> We should keep our roots on, shouldn't we?

Look for what is the Same,

(and different) in form
in structure
in attachment
in coherence
in colour
in length
in thickness
in cross-section
in circumference
in strength
in turgidity
in composition
in arrangement

Keep asking the form-and-function questions.

Use a handlens and note all details:
Do you notice prickles ?

	hairs ?
Where can you find them ?	stings ?
	thorns ?
	fibres ?
	fluff ?
How are they attached ?	vines ?
	scabs ?
	bumps ?
	ridges ?
What function could they have ?	grooves ?
	stripes ?
	holes ?
	pits ?
	rings ?
How many can you find ?	knots ?
	wax ?
	fatty stuff ?
Can you count them ?	stickiness ?
	scars ?
	hooks ?
And what else do you find ?	patterns ?
	spots ?

· Where do the roots go, over to become stem ?

· How is the leaf attached to its stalk (petiole) and the stalk to the stem ?

· How does the stem branch, or grow branches ?

· Where and how are the flowers attached ?

· What shape do the cross-sections of stalks
roots
stems
leaves have ?

· How many colours do you find in a plant ?

II: Every Plant wants to become Something.

Every plant is equipped to germinate,
to grow,
to bloom,
and to reproduce.

But... no plant lives alone
Everywhere there is a struggle for life...

> What does the plant itself tell about its determination to live, to survive and to reproduce?

Structure and form of the whole plant, as well as of any of its parts, reveal something of these functions of survival.

What can you understand of this tale?
--- or make comprehensible?

Go and collect each two entire plants of the same species.

Then make a double piece of work:

On the left:
What does the plant as a whole tell about itself?

On the right:

What does each part contribute to this story? (=natural history)
or: what does each part tell about itself and the whole plant?

Repeat this with another species of plant.

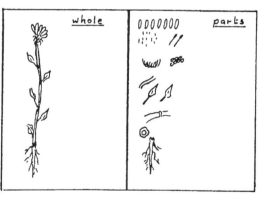

whole | parts

If children use different species of plants, they can arrange their work so that many plants tell their story: let them compare.

Plantwords

It is good for children to collect certain words, names and terms, and become familiar with their meaning and their use, so they can

Terminologia botanica

a) better understand the biology of plants,

b) better remember important details,

c) better distinguish between species, or kinds, when appropriate,

d) better communicate.

There are:

Do-words:
- Mow, grow, sew.
- Bloom
- Bud - - -

Thing-words:
- Berry
- Bud
- Blossom
- Axil
- Vine
- Petiole

Name words:
- Moss
- Fern
- Grass
- Pod
- Petal
- Heather

Names
- Teasel
- Tulip
- Parsnip
...or even
- Capsella bursa pastoris

Children like making their own "plant book" in which, besides gathering all information they want, they can also collect their plant words alongside pictured or preserved plants. Allow them patiently time in plenty to "complete" it to their own satisfaction.

Oh, I never finish! I keep adding fresh pages because I keep finding new words and new plants!

TAKE CARE!

The plants are and remain important. Words only serve.

WHERE
do all those little plants come from?

Any bare patch of ground..
Any dug-up flowerbed...
Any freshly weeded frontgarden...
fills up with little plants in
what seems to be no time... Weeds all over!

Plants
you plant.
Weeds
you weed.

It certainly is a fascinating problem

- Do go and search around your neighbourhood:
  where do you find many plants of one kind
  together?

- Can you find "parent plants" and "offspring"
  growing side by side?
  Do not only look for seedlings,
  try and find runners, too, and
  dig into the ground, gently, around
  fresh shoots.

- Have a close look at a handful of soil.
  Use a handlens. Can you spot seeds?
  Or bulbs? Or rhizomes with nodes? Or...
  · Yes? How many?
  · NO? Well, put a trowelful
        of topsoil in some vessel.
     Keep it moist and warm.
   Cover it —or put it into— a
   plastic bag and look what
   happens in a few days' time.

Go back to where this soil came from and look!

215

Mystery Seeds

 Scrape fresh soil from under your shoes or boots after walking in the "fields" or in the countryside.

Or collect soil from a well-used doormat.

Sprinkle this on top of some soil in an old baking tin, or something. Moisten it and keep it moist and warm --- wait ...
                            patiently ...   °°(perhaps)
and see what grows out of it

Then go out and see if you can find the same plants and look what their seeds are like --- (if you can find any)

Problem!
How can you be sure, or make sure, that the seeds were in the soil that came from your shoes or doormat?

Yes, and not already in the soil in the old baking tin?

Oh, that is simple! Just heat the ---

sshhh...
Let the children talk about it first, and try to find a way out of this problem.

What is a blossom? What is a bloom?

The flower, children, is the reproductive part of the plant which is made up of these parts: Pistil, Stamen, corolla, blah, blah, blah, blah, blah, blah, blah, blah, blah.

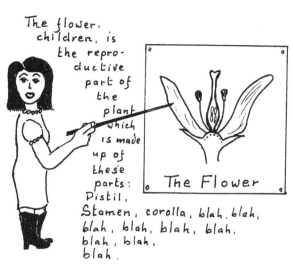

The Flower

This language lesson may be useful, but...

Does "The Flower" exist?

Go and find it in the garden.

Collect a variety of flowers and blossoms. Try and identify those parts in each bloom which seem to have the same function.

Divide a paper so that you can stick or tape or sketch parts of flowers which "belong" together.

Petals	Sepals	Pistil	Stamen	Ovary

Help the children with proper terms when needed. Use pins, (a razor) and hand lenses: tiny flowers are flowers, too.

My mother says her geraniums are good bloomers

Oh, but my Granny wears them.

217

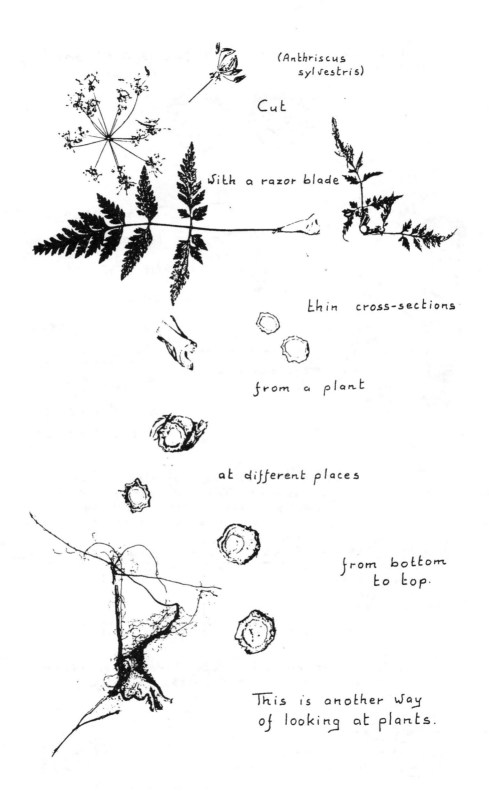

(Anthriscus
sylvestris)

Cut

with a razor blade

thin cross-sections

from a plant

at different places

from bottom
to top.

This is another way
of looking at plants.

Classifying Plants.

oh?

My uncle
Linnaeus
calls that
Taxonomy

What?

Gosh!

Pff.

For this you need quite
a few plants...

Before local frontgardens
get ruined or the floral
environment becomes de-
populated, look for a
convenient piece of ground
where many common plants
occur.

Let children form groups
of five. Each child is to
collect five different plants,
including grasses. This
results in each group
working with 25 plants,
which is enough.

① Divide all plants in _two_
groups.

○ Why do you do it this way?

○ What do the plants in one
group have in common?

○ Does this exclude the opposite
group?

- Briefly describe and
characterize each group.

② Divide the (two) groups
again into two groups

③ Then once more divide
the 4 groups into two..

④ and again ...

⑤ and again ...

Children should talk
and discuss and argue
about their divisions,
for their choice should
be based upon the ans-
wers to the questions:
Why this choice of division?
What do the plants in one
group have in common?

A brief description
characterizing each
group can be written
on a small piece of
paper, or a card,
which then can serve
as a label to each
group of plants.

See following page.

until you cannot divide
a group any more, because
there is only one (kind
of) plant left in it.

I did it
my way.

219

Key

It will be rather difficult for the children in the beginning to spot exclusive characteristics. Talk with them, argue with them, and help them decide.

If the children manage to divide and subdivide their collection into yes/no groups, and to label each group accordingly, they may get something like the following pattern:

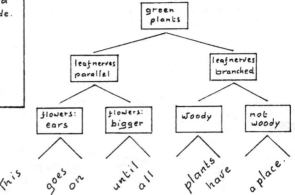

```
                    green
                    plants
            /                   \
     leafnerves            leafnerves
     parallel              branched
     /      \              /        \
flowers:  flowers:      woody      not
 ears     bigger                   woody
```

This   goes on   until all   plants have   a place.

Having done all this "properly", you should have a simple key by which to "identify" the plants in your collection.

Plant Stone?

In the same way you can compose a key to "identify" · autumn leaves
· stones, shells, coins.
· or even the children in the class.

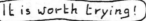

It is worth trying!

Minibeasts and Environment

"Environment" is a very difficult concept, and children only <u>begin</u> to form it.
They need lots of time and plenty of "supporting" experience. Do not attempt to explain it in words. Environment has so much to do with the interaction between living organisms and everything around them, in their immediate surroundings:
- the soil
- the moisture
- the humidity
- the temperature
- the air and the wind
- the weather
  - climate
  - season
  - clouds
  - rain
  - sunshine
- the position of the land and of the (ground) water.
- the prevailing physical features
- the geology
- and all other things living or dead.

But how can children learn this very complex matter?

Go to the ant, thou sluggard, consider her ways, and be wise.

Indeed, whenever children work with minibeasts, they should work with their minibeasts' environment as well:
- Where does it live?
- What is it like there?
  is it dark there, or light?
  cool   or warm?
  moist   or dry?
- Does this minibeast walk?
  or fly?
  or creep, or crawl, or slither?
- Where does it sit down or perch? How?
- Does it dig? Bore? Spin? Build?
- Have you seen it eat? What? How?
- Does it live there where you saw it?
- Does it grow up there?

If you want to keep a minibeast.... can you make <u>a good home</u> for it?

Some more Minibeast-in-environment Questions.

Do the same kinds of minibeasts live and thrive in different places? For instance: flowerbeds, railway embankments, farmland, lawn, road verge, hedgerow, garden, hill top, down, dale, ditch, wood, brook, pool, pond, meadow?

- Or is there something in different places which is the same?

- Or, what is particular to different places where
a) the same minibeasts live?
b) different minibeasts live?

Is it moist or dry? Watery? light or dark? Warm? cool? Overgrown? Open? Screened? Bare?

How wet is wet?
How warm is warm?
How light is light?

How do you measure all this?

Do little beasts, that live in a similar (or in the same) environment, have anything in common? Colour? Shape? Eyes? Skin? Breathing organs? Legs?

· Do little animals change if their environment changes? How?

· What do they do if and when you yourself change their environment?

Does the place tell you anything about the (small) animal(s) that live(s) there?

Does the animal (its structure) tell you anything about its natural environment?

Observing any minibeast: What characteristics make it suited to the place where it lives? What characteristics of the place make it a suitable environment for particular minibeasts ?

You, too, belong to the environment of minibeasts...

Blessing?

or

Doom?

Do they live solitary? In pairs? In groups? Or in multitudes? Who eats whom?

"Our environment is well suited, hey Mama?"

"Yes, dear, but the Club of Rome warns us not to use it up!"

222

<u>Nota Bene:</u>

Observations made by children
are <u>always</u> valuable,
but their "interpretations"
need a little caution...
and so do your own...
and certainly those of schoolbooks.

Conclusions on (e.g.) animal
behaviour, or form and function
relationship, are easily jumped at,
or just taken for granted.

The "Why" and the "how" of animal
behaviour can often be related
to the environment in which
they live, but no more. Nothing
is self-evident.

Nevertheless, children should talk about their
observations and discuss about possible
interpretations, but then in the sphere
of "I think that...", "Could it be that..." : to
hypothesize is fine, because it leads to:
"Shall we try and verify what we think?"

Help the children to base
their "explanations" and
"interpretations" always
on their own observations.

And enhance these observations
by asking answerable questions.

Why does that
caterpillar have
bristles?

And what to think of:
Why has a centipede a
hundred feet?

This is
a good example of
a bad question.
It is not answerable.
For a good question:
Use DO-or LOOK-words:

Write a better
centipede question
below:

What does the caterpillar do
with its bristles?

Are they soft or hard?

223

Chapter 16

Children, mirrors and reflections

Introduction

Mirrors are fascinating things to play with as well as to work with, for they hold an element of magic. Magic and science seem to be at odds, but not necessarily to children. An exploration into the reversed double-world behind the looking glass may well retain something of the thrill of the fairy tale and so provide a strong motivation to pursue some real science. The fairy-tale mirror does not exist in the real word. Every child knows that. But the mirror does and so does a child's wonder about its workings. It doubles whatever is in front of it; it shows you your own face; it makes letters look funny and, at first, illegible; left and right seem confused; it bounces sunlight into a bright spot on the wall; and in combination with another mirror it seems to keep on reflecting reflections infinitely.

Mirrors are universally available and cheap to purchase; children can easily be induced to borrow a mirror from home. Any piece of glass, especially when blackened on one side, makes a workable, though not ideal, mirror. Any shiny, smooth surface can serve as a mirror. In fact, the shape and form of some ordinary shiny things, such as teapots, wheel-hubs, reflectors, Christmas decorations or spoons add to the challenge, for they make things look different.

The activities in this chapter need little introduction to the children: just provide them with mirrors, and slowly structure and order their investigations. It is a unit of learning which entirely depends on the children handling mirrors and other things they need. By direct experience and experimentation children will extract information from the mirrors.

It does not take long for children to start exploring when mirrors are placed in their hands. A certain amount of free exploration, as a 'getting-to-know-you' exercise, is essential. It focuses the children's minds on an area of

225

science; it generates initial questions; it opens a perspective to 'what you would like to know' and . . . they do it anyway. However, free all-over-the-place messing about is still somewhat removed from the scientific inquiry which the children have to learn. The teacher is the one who should bring order and system in the children's explorations and turn them into genuine investigation. Having noticed the children's interest and the direction in which it seems to go, the teacher intervenes. Sometimes the work is stopped altogether and the class discusses possible lines of investigation which have opened up. Sometimes the children are involved enough to be given, individually or in a small working group, a challenge in the form of a problem or a new piece of equipment. Questions and tasks may be given by word of mouth or by an appropriate worksheet. In all cases the work of the children is given more structure, direction and system; it is ready to become more scientific.

This chapter presents a number of ideas for children to investigate various properties of mirrors and how they interact with light. A number of pages (particularly pages 236 to 242) could be copied as they are and given to the children as worksheets. They suggest some problems and indicate how, with the help of one or more mirrors, solutions can be sought. Many of the ideas and tips given on other pages can be transferred to home-made worksheets.

Any unit for children is a teacher's resource. Many ideas and suggestions are given, but they still need the creative teacher to turn them into children's activities or investigations at the right time. Even ready-made worksheets still need the judgement of the teacher as to where and when they should be employed and whether they should, or should not, be adjusted or extended. Worksheets are there to facilitate the work of the teacher; they are aids, tools for the teacher who retains responsibility for ensuring effective learning through the activities. The 'Figure Cards' and 'Sample Cards' described on pages 244 and 245 need to be made by the teacher, after which they can be given to the children to solve the problems they pose. Making sets of these cards is, of course, a very good teacher-training activity. The technical problems of making sets of these cards is slight. Those who cannot draw can use very simple figures, make a stencil or use small stickers. There are so many ways to make this easy that it should put nobody off. Apart from the work of composing pictures-to-be-matched, one is compelled to think. Perhaps there should be 'easy' sets as well as 'tough' sets; what makes a scale of difficulty from simple to hard? Would you include a few cards with an 'impossible' problem (such as the example of a card on the left of page 245)? It would not be bad for the children to realize that in the world of mirrors there are things that just do not work. Mirrors with all their 'magic' obey strict physical laws. A few impossible figure or sample cards may start a lively discussion as well as provide an opportunity to review and summarize the children's findings and ideas so far.

There is no definite sequence in activities provided here. The teacher should use his or her own judgement on what to start with, and on how and with what to continue. The teacher can add activities and inevitably the questions of the children will lead to things not included here. It will be helpful to have other sources and books at hand, and to use them as the occasion arises. Periscopes, lateral inversion and angles of incidence, among others, have been left out because they can be found in every school textbook.

It sounds rather ambitious to expect primary-school children to understand the physics of light and reflection, yet by way of encounter and interaction with mirrors it is entirely possible. Of course, 'reflection' means little or nothing to children unless it is there, present in the mirror they hold in their hand, changing when they change the position of that mirror, or multiplying when they move another mirror nearby. Accumulated experiences, encouraged or suggested by the teacher, ordered and reflected upon in discussion, formulated in words by recording, and given specific meaning as verification of some hypothesis, may order themselves into patterns of understanding; and ideas of a higher level of abstraction may evolve in the minds of the children. They may find that searching behind the looking glass need not be magic in order to be satisfying and rewarding.

CHILDREN,

MIRRORS

AND

REFLECTIONS

JOS ELSTGEEST

These worksheets are about doing with mirrors: about getting children to interact with mirrors. You will not find 'lessons about mirrors' in them. You will not even find any 'useful' information about mirrors. What you will find are a few starters to get children to investigate and solve problems with the help of mirrors.

Once the children are off on their investigations, be prepared for all sorts of questions. Don't let this alarm you, for either: (a) the mirror will provide the answer (and it is good to learn how to ask the mirror); or (b) you know the answer, which makes it easy (well . . . !); or (c) there are books available which provide an answer; or (d) the answer is simply not known by you nor by anybody. Well, let it be so.

Mankind is still learning, and we are not omniscient. That, too, is a very good lesson for our children. Periscopes, lateral inversion, angles of incidence and like bits of language and technology have been left out, for you can find these in every school textbook. So use these terms where appropriate and called for by the interest and questions of the children.

Mirrors and Reflections

What shines and mirrors all around?

This is a good starting question. Many surfaces shine and reflect light, some more, some less than mirrors. All help to understand how light is reflected

Write down five objects, seen from where you sit, and place them in order of "reflectivity"

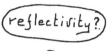

reflectivity?

Could you make a list of "mirror words?
- mirror
- shine
- reflect
- radiate
- bounce
- glisten
- glow
- gleam
- glint
- polish
- sparkle
- image

Look for things which show or do what these words describe.

Examine these objects and try to find words which further explain their reflective qualities, such as:

smooth   glassy
polished   level
burnished   flat
waxed   unruffled
varnished   bald

- clean shave?

This helps children to develop an eye for (relevant) physical properties of things.

Besides... it helps them to discuss sensibly about their observations.

231

Sit around with your children and discuss all together your experiences and observations; raise questions, suggest possible answers, propose experiments and agree on what to do, on who does what, on how to go about it and how it all should be recorded and communicated.

How do things become like mirrors?

Boy! Glass mirrors perfectly! Just look at it from an angle.

Ripples in the water make it a funny mirror. You get a rippleface in it

Spoons and teapots and waterkettles are fine mirrors, like my specs!

And my eyes!

Kitchen foil reflects, but it does not mirror

So do my shoes, provided I have polished them!

Little shiny round things like buttons make things look ever so tiny.

An aquarium is a fine mirror. Look at the surface from below. Everything swims upside down!

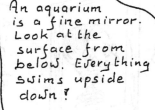

Mirror ?? ɿoɿɿiM

What makes a mirror a mirror?

Oh, but then we need lots of mirrors to do things with!

Why don't you ask the mirror itself?

⌐ That is the way to ask the mirror, so see to it that there are sufficient mirrors available:

Ask the mirror what?

a) Bring some yourself

b) Ask the children to borrow all sorts of mirrors from home: small ones, big ones; mirrors that enlarge or diminish; rear-view mirrors; spoons, coffeepot lids, buttons, christmas decorations, copperplate, buckles, bumpers, as long as it mirrors.

c) Let the children work in groups so they can work with each other's mirrors, and share ideas and experiences.

Questioning, doing, trying, figuring out and renewed questioning will follow naturally.

What follows consists of tips, ideas, suggestions, gentle nudges...
- Some pages may be (photo)copied as worksheets for the children.

Remember: these are only starters! Add and change whatever you want: you and your children are the boss!

Children can do a lot with mirrors

Just give them mirrors

... and watch

In the mirror... you can look at yourself (or others).
you can look round a corner.
you can look in your mouth

With two mirrors you can look behind your ears.

If you hold the mirror above your eyes or your head:

1: everything looks upside down,
2: and in this upside-down world
   - you can walk and jump,
   - shake hands,
   - walk a slalom through a line of chairs or stools,
   - place something in a matchbox
   - and put it on a table.

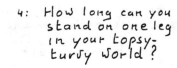

3: You can try and follow a snaky line on the ground.
Draw the line or use a rope or a garden hose.

Rules:
   - never step on it,
   - keep it between your legs,
   - never look at it,
   - unless through the mirror.

4: How long can you stand on one leg in your topsy-turvy world?

234

Try and walk through the schoolbuilding (and out of it by the frontdoor) holding a mirror under your chin: look into the mirror held steady, and facing upward.

Can you make a full face out of a half?

a full one?
face out of
or half

With two mirrors you can ...
Well,

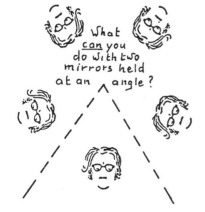

What _can_ you do with two mirrors held at an angle?

Try this:

· Place something small between two mirrors held upright at an angle

· Count the images and measure the angle

· Change the angle and count the images again

· Note what you get
at 180°: - - - - images
90°: - - - - "
60°: - - - - "
45°: - - - - "
30°: - - - - "

· Make this into a simple graph: x angle
        y no. of images

· Can you now figure out a formula which gives you the number of images for any angle?

Look at yourself in this 90° combination...

90°

then wink at yourself.
Can you explain this?

235

WRITE

your name
in mirrorscript

(that is: so that you can
read it in the mirror.)

in blockletters

_____

IN CAPITALS

_____

in handwriting

_____

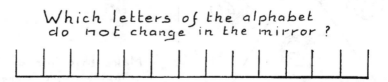

I know a trick
Turn this page
over and hold it
up against the
light

You are allowed to
use tricks, but do
try it without tricks
first.

You may write
"mirrorwords" anywhere:
on paper,
on the floor, the ground,
on the blackboard.

Which letters of the alphabet
do not change in the mirror?

Can you write whole words
which do not change in the
mirror?

_____

... Or a sentence...

_____

Mirrorscrabble

u p s i d e d o w n

A mirror reverts things

That is why mirrorletters look so funny.

laterally

B C D E H I K O X

Hold a mirror on this line to reflect the letters above.

A M
T W
I O
V X
H Y
U

Hold a mirror along this line to reflect the letters on the left.

Can you make a whole word which looks the same in the mirror?   or a sentence?

With the letters above you can write horizontally.

With the letters on the left you may make vertical words.

And... you could make palindromes.

Any idea what a palindrome is?

Oh no!

237

DICK BOXED BEDE

M A M A   I   A M   H O T

Copy this sheet for the children.

Glue the letters on thin cardboard, and cut them out.

Now you can make mirror-scrabble words.

Could you invent a mirror-scrabble-game?

Make up your own rules.

B	B	B	B	C	C	C	C
D	D	D	D	E	E	E	E
H	H	H	H	I	I	I	I
K	K	K	K	O	O	O	O
A	A	A	A	M	M	M	M
T	T	T	T	U	U	U	U
V	V	V	V	W	W	W	W
X	X	X	Y	Y	Y	,	,

How many mice
  can you make with
  · one mirror ?
  · two mirrors ?
  · three mirrors ?
  · more mirrors ?

What difference(s)
  do you see
  when you "multiply"
  the first or
  the second mouse ?

Draw or describe
  a) the position
       of the mirrors.
  b) how the mice are
       sitting.

What more
  can you do
  and find out
  with mice and mirrors?

And what do you get
  · when you mirror
    tiny mice ?
  · or a picture of yourself?
  · or a pencil ?
  · or ...
  · or ...
       you can take anything.

Even with the <u>word</u>
  "mouse" you can
  make something nice
  using two (or more)
  mirrors.

  Try it and draw
  the result.

MOUSE

239

Draw what you can make out of each of these figures and a mirror:

L | S

Lewis Carroll

JABBERWOCKY

'Twas brillig, and the slithy toves
Did gyre and gimble in the wabe:
All mimsy were the borogoves,
And the mome raths outgrabe.

WAUWELWOK

't Wier brodig, en de spiramans
Bedroorden slendig in het zwiets:
Hoe klarm waren de oolgfants,
Bij 't bluijfen der beriets.

Draw the figures (left)
as you will see them
when you place a
mirror on the line.

Only after drawing can you check with
your mirror and see how "correct" you are.

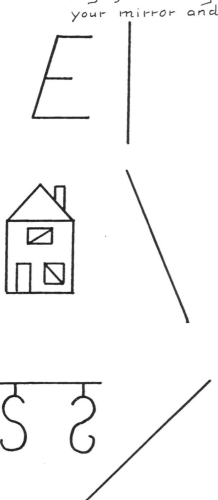

Take a sizeable mirror
and hold it firmly above
your eyes, or high in front,
so that you, looking in the
mirror, look down upon
this paper.
Then follow the instructions underneath.

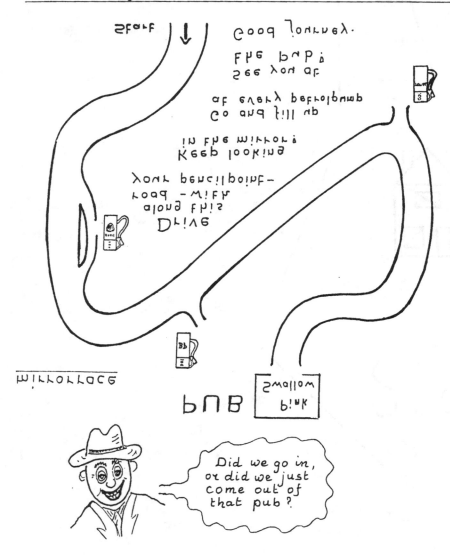

Mirror-work and problem cards

With any picture and any mirror you can make many pictures.

① Paste faces, houses, trees, landscapes, on thin cardboard and see what it becomes when you slide a mirror across it in any direction...

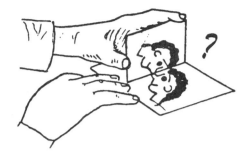

... just for fun ...

...or to challenge one another.

② A real problem card:

Use a mirror and this clock to make:

a) Breakfast time.

b) School time.

c) Dinner time.

d) Bed time.

e) Free time.

f) No time.

or any time

③ Figure Cards

You need one "figure card":

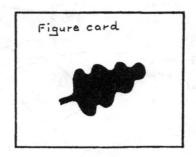

and
a set of problem cards.

The problem is: with which of these cards
— and a mirror — can you
reproduce the figure
on the figure card?

④ Sample card problems

This is another set of problem cards whereby a mirror is used with the "sample card" only.

The problem is: try and copy the configurations found on the other cards. (Can you, or can you not?)

N.B.
These are only a few examples.

You can make many more.

Make various such sets.

Perhaps a nice project for helpful parents..?

famous last words!

The Problem of the Mirrorwall

Imagine you are in a room
one wall of which is one huge
mirror. You are in the company
of a solitary vase of flowers.

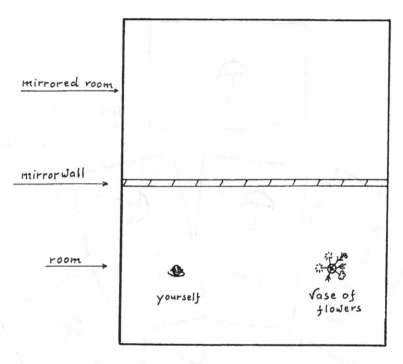

mirrored room →

mirrorwall →

room →

yourself

vase of
flowers

You stand at the spot indicated
on this plan and you are looking
in the mirror at the vase of flowers.

Sketch in pencil the direction
in which you are looking

After drawing your "line
of vision", by all means,
do check with a mirror.
... But do not get
confused.

246

The Problem of the Rear-view Mirror.

Shine or tempest, my car is parked outside.

I had not washed it for quite some time...too long, and so it happened that my rear window looked somewhat grimy...

A naughty little neighbour-boy scribbled on it with a wet finger:

At first I did not notice anything until I boarded my vehicle and looked into my rear-view mirror...

What exactly did I see?

Fill into this mirror image of my rear window what I actually did see.

← rear-view mirror with mirror image of rear-window.

Please, how do you explain this?

_____

_____

_____

247

The Flexible Mirror

Flexible sheets of thin shiny metal or plasticized foil make beautiful flexible mirrors, but these are not easy to obtain.

A sheet of acetate —overhead projector transparency— fixed onto a dark, black, paper makes a very good substitute.

Position yourself facing a source of light (a lamp or a window) and having a darker, shadowy, background, and look at yourself in the flexible mirror.

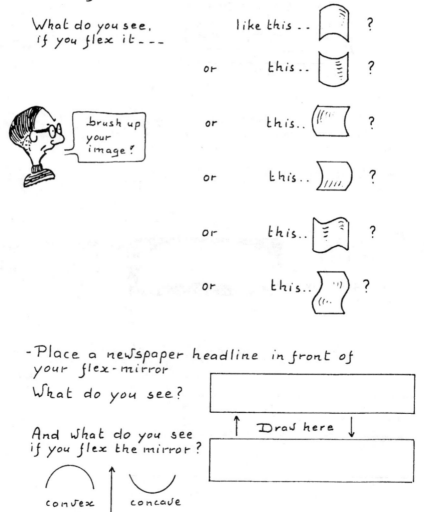

What do you see, if you flex it ___   like this .. ?

or   this .. ?

brush up your image!

or   this .. ?

or   this .. ?

or   this .. ?

or   this .. ?

- Place a newspaper headline in front of your flex-mirror

What do you see?

And what do you see if you flex the mirror?

↑ Draw here ↓

convex | concave

Talking about your work and experiences is very important.

Allow children,
as a matter of course,
to muse and share
ideas and problems.

You can shine the sun from your mirror on to the wall.

How come I am upside-down in a spoon?

From how far?

But you are right side up on the back! Much smaller, though!

Oh, ever so far! And a square mirror shines round!

In the bumper of my dad's car I am awfully fat and ugly. yeagh!

You can play "catch" on the wall. You must try and touch my shiny patch!

You can see the bottom of a fly if you make him walk on a mirror!

I can bounce the sun through your mirror back in my face!

I can look over the heads of grown-ups with my mirror!

Chapter 17

Children and balances

Introduction

Balances are good learning aids in science education and therefore good teaching aids as well. They can be simply made so that children can work with them freely in the classroom. They give children access to some sound science. Not only do children gather some valuable information (so-called 'science facts') in the form of fundamental principles of mechanics (the interplay between forces and movement), they also practise scientific process skills which can lead them beyond these few 'facts' into self-reliant learning and independent thinking.

The title of this chapter has been chosen with a purpose. Children manipulate a balance in order to learn about some of the laws which govern its workings. The condition for learning and understanding is that the children are fully involved: by seeing for themselves, by doing things themselves, by thinking themselves, by verifying things themselves, by making mistakes themselves and by reconsidering their ideas themselves in the light of evidence which they have uncovered themselves.

The children are therefore not given answers before they have had a chance to ask questions. They are confronted with materials that contain a challenge, that raise questions or problems, and that have possible answers within them to be released by thoughtful interaction. The children ask the balances; the balances provide the answers. The teacher helps in the asking as well as in the effort of finding an answer.

The aims of this chapter are to help teachers help children to use balances as a source of information; to 'ask the balance', using scientific process skills; and to generate, through using scientific process skills, the kind of knowledge which leads to further knowledge.

251

How do children use balances as a source of information?

The balance does something in response to something done to it. This makes children's observations of the working of a balance *active* and *selective*. Pushing it down and then letting it go; adding a weight to one side; removing a weight from another side; piling up weights on either side; matching weights to balance; and matching different objects to balance. All these simple actions provide active experiences which leave behind (bits of) ideas on how the balance works.

The first few pages of the chapter suggest that the children do just that. The children's active learning with balances involves thought-processes which are expressed, quite spontaneously, by the children talking. The teacher should, with open ears, make use of this by joining in the talk, either by talking with a child individually or by leading a group discussion about what the children did and what they noticed happening. The active building-up of ideas and concepts while working, together with the co-ordinating exercise of talking about it and discussing findings, soon leads the children to make more general statements on recurring events. Pages 259, 260, and particularly 261, provide examples of this.

It will be found, however, that younger children need much practice before they come up with (or accept) a general abstract statement, such as 'the same volumes of the same substance balance' or 'if A balances B and A balances C, then B balances C also'. Such abstractions may be clear to teachers, but children will tend to try out every instance. We should let them, for this is the way in which they form, test and use patterns.

How do children 'ask the balance'? How do they learn to apply and practise scientific process skills?

If the children just play about with balances without, somewhere along the line, being given some order and direction, they will probably make some interesting discoveries, but learn little science. It is the teacher's task to introduce some order, or some system, into the children's work, by helping them to make the appropriate next step forward when they come to it. The discussions among the children themselves and, more so, the discussions with their teacher, provide ample opportunity to ask the right question at the right time, or to make a suggestion for further activity in order to find more or better answers from the balance. Questions which the children ask themselves or which they adopt from their teacher are an inducement to learning and a strong motive to make an effort, to investigate, to take care to be accurate and not to give up before some understanding has been acquired.

The scientific process skills which the balances invite the children to practise are accurate observation, classifying objects, calculating, comparing quantities, manipulating materials (and instruments) deftly, some designing and making, finding patterns and relationships and, above all, the raising of motivating questions.

The use of these skills, made more conscious by discussion, brings order and purpose in the actions the children undertake. Creating this order and discipline in handling things, creates order in the concepts, ideas and thought-processes which generate from these experiences. For examples one can turn to pages 261 to 264, while the point is underlined by the true story on page 265. The last six pages, of course, should be considered, too.

How does the practice of scientific process skills lead to a kind of knowledge which generates further knowledge?

The more elaborate exercise round the question 'What makes the balance balance?', which is suggested on pages 266 to 270, has proven to be a powerful illustration of how science – via accurate observations and careful recording – can lead to a short-cut towards learning. After having defined, on page 266, some unit of weight or mass (paper-clip) and a unit of distance from the fulcrum (the distance between holes in a strip of pegboard), there are a dozen or so definite simple problems to solve with the help of the balance. Confirmation of the right solution is given by the balancing balance and the outcome is systematically recorded according to the suggested scheme and outline.

Invariably, someone somewhere along the activity will go beyond the simple trial-and-error approach and replace it by predicting what to do; a simple calculation is made and verified. In fact the formula 'Weight times distance on the left equals weight times distance on the right' (or any more sophisticated formulation of the law of moments) is being applied long before students are able to put it accurately into words. Soon a discussion develops around the question: 'What makes a balance balance? What is in equilibrium? The units of weight or mass on either side?' 'No.' 'Or has it to do with their position in relation to the fulcrum?' 'Yes and no.' Soon the proper relationship is worked out and can be expressed in words. At first the students may formulate this relationship in a rather roundabout way, but they will be able to exemplify it by using the numbers they filled in on their record. This shortens it, and from here it is only a small step towards a simple formula which corresponds with the words as well as with the figures $\Sigma(M \times D) = \Sigma(M \times D)$. (Which means that the sum of the units of mass times their distance from the fulcrum on the left arm equals the sum of the units of mass times their distance from the fulcrum on the right arm.)

Provided students, or older children, have had sufficient experience and have made clear records, they can either come up themselves with, or understandingly accept, this formula or its descriptive summary. It is precisely this knowledge which generates new knowledge: new problems can now be solved. The formula allows a short-cut. When an unknown element is then introduced, it can be worked out by simple experimentation and calculation, as the exercises suggested on page 271 indicate.

When the activities are carried out by student teachers, there is a double benefit. They learn or revise some fundamental principles of the physics of balances, which gives them confidence. They also analyse the scientific processes they undergo or apply, which helps them appreciate the process-based teaching which they may be asked to use in their work with children.

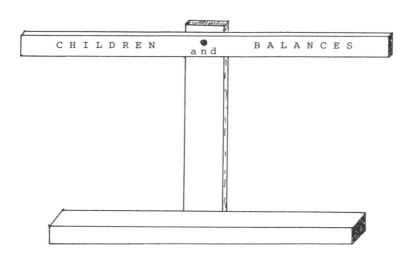

CHILDREN and BALANCES

Jos Elstgeest

A gentle word of caution in advance

A balance is an instrument to do something with.

Only by doing something with it can one investigate its working, and so begin to understand some of the laws which govern it.

Because it is an instrument for doing, it can be placed in the hands of children, and thus it will invite them to interact, that is to explore, to investigate, to experiment and so gain experience. For our primary-school children this is sufficient. Investigation turns their minds into the fertile ground in which later understanding and more correct formulation can flourish.

Therefore, do not force anything upon the children at first. There is nothing yet to be learned by heart, but there is much to be learned by experience. Somewhere along the line learning by heart becomes useful, perhaps, but then they will understand why, and submit to it gladly.

There are simple laws of mechanics (the interplay of forces and movement) which can be discovered by simple investigation and experimentation. By merely manipulating simple balances children discover elementary relationships and these are all they can handle. Our abstract patterns are often beyond them. Primary-school children can manipulate things that work: balances. They have difficulty in handling our generalizations. We must give them time and opportunity to form their own generalizations out of their own experiences.

We can help them on their way by letting them work with balances, freely exploring at first, but gradually with more direction and purpose. The satisfaction of the experiences and the budding conception of what makes the balance balance, guarantee a solid foundation as a basis for reliable understanding when later abstract thinking gives meaning and coherence to observations and experiences.

What follows is a number of ideas on how to work with children and balances. There are no 'lessons on weighing', nor is there a treatise on 'the Law of Moments'. You may add and substitute what you like, as long as it helps you to start a lively interaction between children and balances.

What is a balance?
What does it do?
How does it work?
How does my balance work?
How do I work with my
balance?

equal?
equality?
equilibrium?

Shall I ask
my teacher?

on of the for...
...bout an axis is genera...
...rotation is called negative.
In Fig. II-40 the vector sum...
...lever is obviously zero. What is t...
...ther point? Let us choose the rig...
...ich to find the torques, or as it is ...
Torque of $\vec{F}_1$ is 5 × 0.70 = 3...
...que of $\vec{F}_2$ is 5 × 0.30 = ...
...of $\vec{F}_*$ is 5 × 0.50 = ...
...$\vec{F}_3$ is 15 × 0.5...

a simple lever which...
...) of 5 N, which we locate...
..., each of 5 N. There is only one ...
15 N to balance all the downwar...
...will note that $\vec{F}_1$ and $\vec{F}_2$ are equally...
...er these conditions, the lever is i...
...er from the center without shift...
...be in equilibrium? The sum...

No!
I think I'd
better
ask
my
balance!

A balance is a
fascinating instru-
ment for children
to work with:

It "does" something
in response to what
you do to it your-
self.

It does what I want, provided
I know what it can do and what it
is that I want!

257

Would you like to

<u>Ask the Balance?</u>

Then first make a balance.

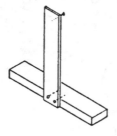

Use a
- small piece of wood,
- a small slat
- a hammer and
- some nails.

These drawings show how to fix things.

We can do it easily

See that there are enough balances: at least one between two children. Working in threes is also good: it enlivens discussion.

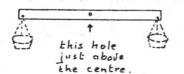

Add a strip of peg-board, two rows wide, and with an odd number of holes in each row.

Look then!

It balances

It doesn't

But a thin strip of wood (a slat) with a few holes makes a good balance arm, too.

Do not under-estimate this very simple instrument: it is sensitive to small fractions of a gramme

this hole just above the centre.

With the younger children

there is little to fuss about.

Make sure that there
are some balances
freely available ... together with
blocks, acorns,
beans, washers,
and assorted odds and ends.

Let them explore as they wish:
this is a first "encounter",
leading to a first dialogue: "What are you?"
"What can you do?"
These basic questions "What do you do?"
are sufficient for them.
Watch and learn from children
and balances alike.

Miss!
It goes down!

Look! It
sits
crooked.

It tilts
when I
take
something
off.

First it
seesaws
and then
it sits still.

Short story.

Yulitha and Dominic are together working on the
same little balance. Yulitha notices that the
heavier side of the balance moves down. She adds
a weight to the other side which now moves down.
Soon she is satisfied with this observation and
changes to something else. Dominic, however,
notices that some weights cause the arm to dip
only a little way, while other weights make it
swing all the way down. This fascinates him and
he continues to explore this further by trying
out a multitude of different objects.

This shows that not all children do the same thing
when they are working on the same thing.

259

Making Equilibrium.

Somewhat older children begin to relate the behaviour of the balance to what they put on it. They start to compare, and now their balance becomes an instrument for making equilibrium.

With nothing on it, it sits straight. I can make it sit straight with beans on it!

"Sitting straight." We call: "being in equilibrium."

"Making equilibrium" now becomes the end of the children's endeavours. They like practising this skill by making all sorts of things balance each other.

Two chestnuts are in equilibrium with five acorns.

Making equilibrium we just call: balancing.

My bolt and nut make equilibrium with seven washers.

Their trials are direct and concrete, which helps the children develop objectivity in observation.

But "general rules" are not (yet) made, nor used.

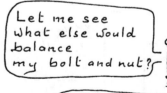

Let me see what else would balance my bolt and nut?

I shall try it

Oh look, my bolt and nut balance my rubber!

Then, of course your rubber also balances seven washers.

... but that is not so obvious to this child!

From Balancing to Weighing.

Our modern grocers no longer weigh their wares on proper balances. Instead they use some electronic gadget. Our children do not always associate weighing with balancing.

Four nuts balance a tangerine

Four nuts also balance my scissors

) think when two things are of equal weight, they keep the balance always in equilibrium

Then the tangerine must also balance the scissors.

This, at least, is true for the equal arm balance.

Once the children reach this notion, they can start weighing things with their simple balances.

Sir, where are the weights?

Look for your own weights. Washers are fine units of weight, they'll do.

What is not a balance?

Take a twig,
    a knife,
    a board,
    a stick,
    a broom,
    a shoe,
    a ruler,
    a straw,
    a stiff wire,
    a spoke,
    a pencil,
    a bar of chocolate,
    a clotheshanger,
    a no matter what;

My specs, my chair, my spoon

add a piece of string in the proper
position, and you make it into a balance!

With sticks   or   straws
    strings   or   threads
    cut-outs or   things
and patience and devotion,
you can make a balance
which balances a balance
which balances a balance!

This is called

    a mobile.

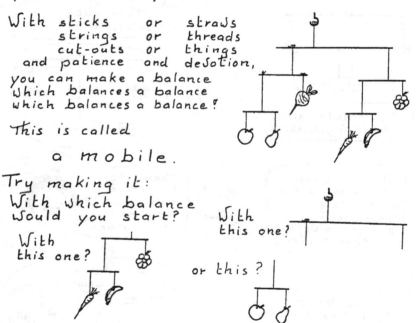

Try making it:
With which balance
would you start?

With
this one?

With
this one?

or this?

Children who can solve these little
problems begin to understand quite
a bit of the working of a balance.

    So, why not let them do so?

Balancing Boards.

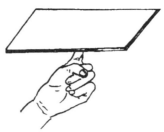

Can you balance
a sheet of cardboard
on the tip of your
finger?

Try this: • Make a simple
plumb-line:
attach a small weight
to the end of a piece
of thin string or
a thread.
Suspend this from
a hook or nail in
the wall.

• Punch 3 holes in your rectangular
sheet of cardboard in three
different places.
(The 3rd hole is a control.)

• Unbend a paperclip into a hook.
(Twist the bottom part forward by 90°)

• Hook on your card-
board and hang it
behind the plumb-
line on the wall.

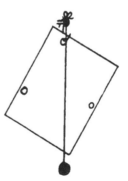

• Carefully indicate
how the plumb-line
runs across the
board.

• Repeat all this using
the other two holes.

You can mark the vertical
plumb-line by carefully placing two
dots, just underneath the weighted
string. By joining the dots with pencil
and ruler, you draw a good straight line.

What do these plumb-lines tell you?

- What do they tell you about "equilibrium"?

 Notice that the hole from which you suspend your cardboard is a fulcrum, a pivot, a turning-point... just like the centre hole of a balance...

- How would the areas on both sides of the plumb-line compare?

- Is it a matter of area?

- What is the importance of the point where the lines cross?

 What happens if I stick my chewing gum at the backside?

- From where to where, do these lines run?

- Place the crossing-point now on the tip of your finger...

 Can you balance it on the tip of your finger?

Note:
The point where the lines cross is called: Point of Gravity or Centre of Gravity. Could you call it "Point of Equilibrium"?

Cut your card into an irregular shape. Repeat the plumb-line experiment.

Do the same questions apply?

Stick a weight somewhere on the edge.

Could you find the centre of gravity... of a soup plate? a shoe? a knife? a handkerchief?

or... your own?

 I am nothing but a centre of gravity!

A short story

The children of a fifth grade at Vikundu, a village in the United Republic of Tanzania, worked with balances for quite some time. One of their activities was to compare various objects which they had found in and around their school, such as stones, blocks of wood, lumps of clay, dry bones, pieces of metal, fruit and inkpots. They started to arrange these things in order of weight. First they arranged them by feeling only, without using their balance. When they later checked their 'feeling', they had to make some adjustments.

These children spoke Swahili, and they used the most common word, '*Uzito*' to describe literally 'heaviness'. The concepts of 'weight' as something measurable, or 'mass' as a physical property of substances, had not yet been considered or named. Yet the problem of 'heavy but small' as compared with 'light but big' did arise spontaneously, first as an observation, but soon as an object of wonder and amazement. The bolt and nut (inseparably rusted together) was small but much heavier than a big dry bone. It even beat a block of wood on the balance! How is this possible?

Although solving this problem was not forced upon them, it kept their minds busy, because soon one little boy with a deep thinking furrow upon his brow declared that the 'heaviness' of the iron bolt and nut must be closely packed together, closer than the 'heaviness' of a bone or of wood. The bolt and nut of smaller dimension can therefore have more 'heaviness' than the bigger bone or block of wood.

Then the boy was allowed to explain his theory to the other children and they were asked to try to find some word or expression which would neatly describe this property. This was quite a linguistic proposition, but it set little wheels turning in their heads, and they came up with a surprisingly original term. They called it '*Uzito wa Asili*'. Literally translated this means 'heaviness of origin', the natural heaviness of things. What a beautiful example of trying to put an observation and its consequent concept sensibly into words! Would our 'density' be so much better?

The "Law" of the balance:
or: What makes the balance balance?

The following course of action can be undertaken by older children.

By solving some simple, direct problems — to which the balance "knows" the answers — you are led to a general conclusion: a generalization, a rule, a law, which can be expressed in a formula. (This process is called: induction.)

Understanding this formula enables you to solve new problems by deduction.

Provide enough balances with a peg-board strip as balance arm, suspended from the centre, top hole.

| 0 0 0 0 0 0 0 0 0 0 0 0 0 0 0 0 0 0 0 0 0 0 0 0 0 0 0 0 0 |
| 14 13 12 11 10 9 8 7 6 5 4 3 2 1 0 1 2 3 4 5 6 7 8 9 10 11 12 13 14 |
| 0 0 0 0 0 0 0 0 0 0 0 0 0 0 0 0 0 0 0 0 0 0 0 0 0 0 0 0 0 |

Number the holes as shown above. These numbers indicate the distances (D) measured from the centre (0). This is the fulcrum, or turning-point. (The number of holes may be 14, 12, or 10.)

Use sturdy paperclips as "weights", as units of mass. One paperclip is 1M.

Per hole you can use more than one unit of mass: e.g. you are instructed to place "3M at D8".

This means that you must place 3 paperclips in hole no. 8. (Left or right as the case may be.)

For hanging paperclips it is better to use the holes in the bottom row of your peg-board.

Before you start, make a small rider out of bent wire, or a tiny paperclip, so that you can bring your balance arms into perfect equilibrium: only then can your balance give you faultless answers.

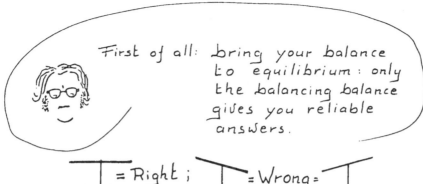

First of all: bring your balance to equilibrium: only the balancing balance gives you reliable answers.

⊥ = Right ;   ⊤ = Wrong = ⊤

these are examples of what to do and how to record it: Put 1 unit of Mass at Distance 14, on the left side, and 1 unit of M. at D. 14 on the right-hand side.

This is one problem !

	Left		Right	
	M	D	M	D
	1	14	1	[14]
	[2]	6	1	[12]
	2	4	[1]	8
1)	1	14	2	[ ]
2)	2	14	1	[ ]
			[ ]	4
3)	[ ]	10		
	1	[ ]	3	11
4)	3	[ ]	2	12

267

Mind: What has been written **must** be done; do that first. Then figure out what makes the balance balance... and fill in the blanks.

Left		Right	
M	D	M	D
5) 2	□	□	5
1	9	2	14
6) □	9	□	12
□	7		
□	5		
2	3		
7) □	13	1	9
3	□	□	□
8) 1	□	□	10
2	□	3	11
3	5	□	12

Now much is left to your own ingenuity; the recorded results may well differ one from the other, but if the balance is in equilibrium, the "answer" must be right. Do you agree?

Left		Right	
M	D	M	D
3	5	☐	13
☐	☐	☐	☐
☐	11		
2	☐	2	11
☐	☐		
4	☐	☐	15
☐	☐	2	☐
☐	☐	☐	☐
☐	☐	☐	☐
		☐	☐

Do we have to go the long way?

No, let us take a short cut.

Ask yourself: - When is there equilibrium?
- In what way does left equal right? What is the meaning of $L = R$?
- On what does equilibrium depend?
  · on the total units of mass?
  · on the distance(s) of the mass(es) from the fulcrum?
  · Or on both?

- If both M and D influence the state of equilibrium, how then are they related?

Can you express this in a simple formula?

Do remember this well, because with the help of this formula and a balance you can now solve many problems that you could not solve before.

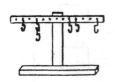

Problem 1 Use the formula to establish the "weight" (or mass) of these scissors.

(Use the paperclip as a unit of mass).

Problem 2 Find the "weight" (mass) of whatever you find in your pocket:
- knife
- pen
- comb
- lipstick
- doesn't matter what

Problem 3 Find with the help of _not more_ than _4_ paperclips (four!) the exact mass of a ball of clay (or plasticine)

Problem 4 What does a pin weigh?

Problem 5 Establish the mass of your balance arm ...

but _without_ using another balance.

Problem 6 You have a broom
a string
and a 100 grammes weight ...

Use this device to weigh a kilo of sugar.

ED.91/D.187/A